EDITING EIGHTEENTH-CENTURY TEXTS

EDITING EIGHTEENTH-CENTURY TEXTS

Papers given
at the Editorial Conference
University of Toronto, October 1967

EDITED BY D.I.B. SMITH

Published for the Editorial Conference Committee,
University of Toronto
by University of Toronto Press

Printed in Canada
SBN 8020 3223 0

Contents

Contributors

G. E. BENTLEY, JR., professor of English, University College, University of Toronto, was educated at Princeton University and the University of Oxford. He is the author of *The Early Engravings of Flaxman's Classical Designs* (1964) and has compiled, with M. K. Nurmi, *A Blake Bibliography* (1964). He has edited Blake's *Vala or The Four Zoas* (1963) and *Tiriel* (1967). His "Blake Records" is shortly to be published by the Clarendon Press.

THEODORE BESTERMAN is director of the Institut et musée Voltaire, Geneva. It would be quite impossible here to list Dr. Besterman's many distinctions and numerous and diverse publications. Of most importance for us is his monumental 107-volume edition of *Voltaire's correspondence* (1953–1966).

O M BRACK, JR., associate professor of English, is director of the University of Iowa Center for Textual Studies. He is textual editor for the bicentennial edition of the *Works of Tobias Smollett*, assistant editor of *Books at Iowa*, and one of the compilers of "English Literature, 1660–1800: A Current Bibliography" published annually in *Philological Quarterly*. With Walter

Barnes he is editing an anthology, *Bibliography and Textual Criticism: English and American Literature 1700 to the present,* for the Patterns of Literary Criticism series. His edition of the poetry of Michael Wigglesworth is to be published shortly.

DONALD GREENE, Leo S. Bing professor of English, University of Southern California, has degrees from the University of Saskatchewan, the University of London, and Columbia University. He is the author of *The Politics of Samuel Johnson* (1960) and editor of *Samuel Johnson: A Collection of Critical Essays* (1965). He is a member of the editorial committee of the *Yale Edition of the Works of Samuel Johnson* and editor of a forthcoming volume of Johnson's political writings in that edition.

JOYCE HEMLOW, is Greenshields professor of English Language and Literature at McGill University, Montreal. She is the author of *The History of Fanny Burney* (1958) which was awarded the James Tait Black Memorial Book Prize for the best biography of the year, the Governor General's Medal for academic non-fiction, and the Rose Mary Crawshay Prize. With Jeanne M. Burgess and Althea Douglas she has compiled the recently published *Catalogue of the Burney Family Correspondence 1748–1878*. She is editor of the forthcoming "Letters and Journals of Fanny Burney (Madame d'Arblay)."

WILLIAM J. HOWARD, assistant professor, St. Michael's College, University of Toronto, was educated at the University of Toronto and Leeds University. He has published on such widely diverse subjects as Pope, Mittelholzer, and African studies, and is the author of a forthcoming book on the publishing industry of the early eighteenth century. He is the convener for the 1968 Conference on Editorial Problems.

EDITING EIGHTEENTH-CENTURY TEXTS

Introduction

D.I.B. SMITH

The editor's education is an education in humility, precisely paralleling the education of the critic. The youthful critic starts out full of enthusiasm for the metaphor of the judge: it is he who has been singled out to evaluate the greatest writers of the past, to decide precisely what in them is relevant to our concerns and what must be considered the relative failures in their achievement. Many bitter years later he discovers that if he judges he will be judged and not favourably: that the person the critic criticizes is not the poet but himself and that his function is to interpret his poet and pass judgement only on his own ignorance and insensitivity. The ultimate aim of the critic, teacher and editor alike is to become a transparent medium for whatever one criticizes, teaches or edits.

With this stern reflection on the corruption latent in absolute editorial powers, Professor Northrop Frye welcomed the delegates to the third Conference on Editorial Problems at the University of Toronto. Like its predecessors the conference was organized around a particular period – in this case the latter half of the eighteenth century – and offered a forum in which editors and those interested in editing, could discuss their problems.

The papers were delivered on the evening of October 27 (following a reception given by the Oxford University Press and dinner at Massey College) and on the morning and afternoon of the 28th.

If Professor Frye was worried about purity of text, his auditory were no less concerned – both Dr. Besterman and Miss Hemlow dealt with complex problems of restoration. For the editor of Voltaire's letters these difficulties are multiplied a hundred-fold by the staggering abundance of the output. The sheer size of the edition, as Dr. Besterman shows, was the crucial problem on which almost all other decisions were contingent. Voltaire's contemporaries must have feared, as John Hall did of William Prynne, that he "like a Leviathan would swallow up all the Paper, and be a means to raise Ballads and Pamphlets from three farthings to a penny a Sheet."

Miss Hemlow indicated some of the obstacles in recovering the original state of Fanny Burney's letters and journals after three generations of excision and revision. It is interesting to note that had Miss Burney's own revisions been to her novels, they doubtless would have been respected, even critically celebrated, but documents must be presented to the reader in their pristine form, without second thoughts or prudent modification. Indeed, authorial revision may be regarded as a special problem for the editor of eighteenth-century letters. The self-conscious epistle and the public private-letter were characteristic of the age.

Professor Bentley's paper was read by a deputy as wisps of snow drifted out of a leaden Toronto sky, and its author luxuriated in the African sun. He was concerned with the formidable editorial difficulties raised by the unique nature of Blake's illuminated printing. Here, since no pattern of revision emerges from the differing copies, one of the central problems is descriptive; the editor must search out and give a precise account of every known example of Blake's work.

The bounds of William Strahan's publishing empire were

almost identical with those of eighteenth-century English literature itself; he published Johnson, Fielding, Thomson, Gibbon, Hume, Robertson, and Smollett. As a member of parliament for the borough of Malmesbury, he had as his colleague the celebrated Charles James Fox, and his prosperity, indicated by the fact that "he kept his coach," was, as Boswell observed, "a good topick for the credit of literature." But his greatest significance for posterity will probably arise from the detailed and scrupulous printing ledgers which he kept. Professor Brack's paper was an introduction to the ledgers with an account of some of the difficulties experienced in getting them to yield up their treasures. This paper was followed by the liveliest discussion of the conference, in which the relative merits of different modes of presenting the information in the ledgers was vigorously debated. Most delegates favoured typographic reproduction with reorganization of the material rather than an indexed facsimile.

Father Howard's paper was a welcome – even necessary – excursion, moving away from the narrowly technical concerns of editing to the worlds of legal history and criticism. He charted the rise in the status of *originality* in literature, together with the complementary discrediting of the formerly dominant concept of *imitation* as these are shown in the struggle to establish a new definition of copyright in the last quarter of the eighteenth century.

No consideration of the problems of editing texts from this period could be complete without touching on the difficulties in dealing with the work of Samuel Johnson. It was not possible to have a paper on Johnson at the conference but, happily, Professor D. J. Greene agreed to give us an insight into the workings of the monumental Yale edition. Not only does this paper cover a vital area of editing, but it affords a useful continuity with the reviews of other massive group projects – the Toronto Mill and the Yale More – that were a central feature of the earlier volumes in this series. It is also appropriate that this paper conclude the collection, for Johnson's works pose almost every conceivable problem that can face an editor. His output was incredibly diverse, ranging through all forms of printed expression with the possible exception of graffiti. The difficulty of establishing a canon is immense, probably insurmountable, while the attendant problem of how much to print of what is not certainly Johnson's, is equally incapable of facile solution. The obstacles are awesome, as Professor Greene demonstrates, and yet we desperately need a good edition of Johnson.

Readers of these papers may find it curious that editions of the two great men of letters dealt with here – Voltaire and Johnson – whose works so clearly needed to be made available in an incorrupt and useful form, should have had such difficulty in attracting the support of foundations or the interest of publishing houses. Perhaps some light will be cast on this question at the fourth conference to be held at Toronto in November of this year, under the direction of Father Howard, when we shall be laying aside the chronological focus of the previous conferences to examine the topic "Author and Publisher."

The broad lines of the third conference were laid down by Professor G. E. Bentley, Jr. When he somewhat unexpectedly left for a year at the University of Algiers as Fulbright lecturer, the practical arrangements were taken over by the present writer. What success we have had has come from the noble assistance of the Committee,* the financial aid of the University of Toronto and the Canada Council, and the wit and grace of the speakers.

*Members of the Committee for 1967 were G. E. Bentley, Jr., David Esplin, Francess Halpenny, W. J. Howard, J. A. McClelland, J. M. Robson, R. J. Schoeck, and D. I. B. Smith.

Twenty Thousand Voltaire Letters

THEODORE BESTERMAN

I HAVE OFTEN BEEN asked to say something about my edition of *Voltaire's correspondence* but I have always declined, for the first person singular is not my favourite pronoun. Nor is it much easier to talk about the book itself, for it is not the product of one of those great scholarly factories for which this continent is famous. It is, on the contrary, so deeply personal a work that it and I are barely distinguishable, except physically: an ingeniously malicious friend has pointed out that the published *Voltaire's correspondence* is heavier than its editor and, if piled up, much taller. Besides, waiving such material considerations, the work has special aspects the merest reference to which sounds like a boast.

However, having now yielded to your flattering invitation, there is nothing for it but to go the whole hog. I therefore declare at once that *Voltaire's correspondence* is the biggest project of its kind ever published or even attempted, and that it was planned, performed, and published in only twenty years. Just before the printing began the manuscript filled very tightly six four-drawer filing cabinets. The book extends to 107 volumes, in which are published over 20,000 letters; about 200,000 notes; nearly 400 appendixes containing documents, excursuses, long notes, and the like; and well over 500 illustrations. The general index extends to over 3,200 columns, in five volumes; the bibliography of the correspondence fills nearly 400 columns, since Voltaire letters were printed for the first time in about 2,000 distinct publications; the calendars of manuscripts of the letters and related documents provide inventories of material found in nearly 400 archives, libraries, and other collections in many parts of the world; the list, *vulgariter* called bibliography, of works cited in the notes fills an entire volume; the apparatus includes also a list of unidentifiable, spurious, doubtful, and lost letters; a key to pseudonyms and nicknames; an author index of the passages quoted by Voltaire from numerous writers in many languages; a concordance; and a list of all the letters, arranged alphabetically by correspondents. And I must add that there exist in typescript two valuable but very voluminous aids which I was obliged to omit: an index of incipits and a chronology of Voltaire's life, each of which would fill an entire volume.

Pray do not imagine for a single moment that I am guilty of the vulgar error of regarding quantity as in itself a quality: it is simply an all-important factor. I have to mention these details, for I cannot talk intelligibly about *Voltaire's correspondence* without specifying them. Let me assure you, however, that I am my own severest critic, and that whatever I say about my work is said quite impersonally.

You will now appreciate that it was not by chance that I chose the title "Twenty thousand Voltaire letters." It is in fact intended to emphasize at the outset that nearly all the editorial problems connected with this publication, and indeed most of its problems of whatever kind, were dominated by the size of the project.

It is hardly necessary to point out that the most acute of all the difficulties presented by a publication of these dimensions is that of money. I could say a great deal about this, but as it is only indirectly an editorial problem I will limit myself to a few words, and leave the rest to smoulder painfully in my subconscious. In brief: I was never able to obtain any financial help from any foundation towards the cost of publication. I did have one editorial assistant for about eight years, that is, for less than half the time the work was in progress, and this assistant's salary was paid by the Fonds national suissse de la recherche scientifique. Apart from that the whole of the work was undertaken and published at my own expense[1] and single-handedly, with the help of one secretary.

This was partly the result of some distressingly circular thinking on the part of the foundations. Before I started work I was told that the undertaking was impossibly ambitious, that I could never carry it through, and that any money given for it would therefore be wasted. After I had done all the preliminary work, and even published a few volumes, I tried again, and I was then told that as I could apparently manage on my own I might as well go ahead on that basis. It is easy to laugh now, but I did not laugh then, for this queer logic meant that in order to edit *Voltaire's correspondence* I of course had to do the work, which was a pleasure; and sink in it a large part of my worldly goods, which was not unbearably disagreeable; but I also had to become a publisher and a financier, and that I resented and still resent.

It seems to me that the attitude of the foundations needs to be thoroughly revised. I proposed at one time that a certain number of copies of the publication be bought for distribution to libraries which could not afford a book which is necessarily expensive, or which could afford only one copy. This was turned down with contumely. Why? Is this not a highly appropriate way of helping all concerned? If the sale of *Voltaire's correspondence* could have been increased by even a hundred sets, the price, to say nothing of my financial burden, could have

1 / Except for a small but welcome contribution, at the end, from the state and city of Geneva.

been reduced to an appreciable extent, and the benefit would thus have been spread, beyond the immediately benefiting libraries, to all subscribers, and even to the wretched editor-publisher-financier. Printing costs are going up all the time: the last text-volume of *Voltaire's correspondence* (that is, apart from the particularly expensive indexes and bibliographies) cost me 140 per cent more per page than the first volume, and of course I could not increase the price by anything remotely like that percentage. We are now quickly approaching a situation in which scholars will be able to get money to do their research (though I got none), the results of which will then remain unpublished. I often meet this situation as a publisher. The 60 or so volumes so far issued, or in the works, of the *Studies on Voltaire and the eighteenth century* – which I edit and publish at the Institut et musée Voltaire – include about twenty valuable studies for which publishing grants could not be obtained, or only on a quite inadequate scale, and which I therefore had to subsidize if they were not to remain unpublished. The same thing is true of R. A. Leigh's remarkable edition of Rousseau's correspondence, which I am also publishing at the Institut Voltaire.

There was and is a further difficulty, so painful to contemplate that I will merely mention it: nationalistic prejudice.

For the strictly editorial problems I encountered, there was no precedent: all had to be thought out *ab ovo*, and worked out in the most minute detail. And this had to be done once and for all: there can be no second thoughts in a work of this size.

To bring this home let me offer one detail which at first sight will appear quite trivial: the form to be adopted for the heading of each letter. Because of the number of letters involved, the great extent of time during which they were written – seventy years – the fact that I had recovered correspondence with over 1,700 persons, and the closely knit structure of French society in the eighteenth century, similar names occur over and over again. There are, for instance, several members of the same families, of different generations and branches, who are impossible to distinguish without full particulars. Thus at the beginning of the alphabet I find three Amelot, four Argens or Argence, four Argenson, three Argental. It was therefore advisable, in order to avoid misunderstanding and much unnecessary expenditure of energy by the reader, to give the correspondent's name in full each time, and this is what I finally decided to do. But it was only after prolonged hesitation, because this decision meant that the space occupied by each letter was on the average increased by the equivalent of three text-lines, or sixty thousand lines in all – equivalent to 1,500 pages. When such consequences flow from trivial details, you will appreciate the minute planning that had to go into the more important aspects of this project, and particularly the more substantial editorial decisions. For instance, to take what is still a relatively minor instance, Voltaire's correspondence is so thick with allusions of every kind that if each reference which could bear explanation had in fact been annotated, the entire publication would have run, at a guess, to three hundred volumes. And you will appreciate what this means: it does not mean merely that the edition would have been absurdly large and costly; it means in reality that it could never have been undertaken or, if undertaken, could never have been completed. It was therefore necessary from the beginning to determine very precise principles, and to work out their practical implications in the utmost detail. In the most general terms, I decided to annotate in such a way as to make it as easy as possible for a scholar to follow up any particular aspect or detail in which he is interested at any given moment, but to avoid doing all his homework for him in advance.

One more preliminary consideration was very important to me. I have always been passionately interested in typography, and I was determined to produce as handsome a book as I could. I decided on the Baskerville typeface, chiefly of course because it is handsome and legible, and was designed in the eighteenth century, but also because Voltaire had had some correspondence with Baskerville himself, and because Beaumarchais had acquired the Birmingham printer's matrices for the great Kehl edition. I then worked out a layout which would permit each letter to be read without interruption, but also without in any way sacrificing the scholar's requirements. This was achieved, among other things, by grouping all the notes, in two columns, at the end of each letter. On looking back after twenty years I still feel sure that this is the best way of tackling the problem. In fact, when Dr. Leigh and I planned the layout of his Rousseau correspondence, we were unable to devise any improvement.

Some people – fortunately few – have criticized *Voltaire's correspondence* for being a luxurious edition. This is quite untrue, and it is sad that there are a few sciolists (disciples, no doubt, of Madison Avenue) who cannot distinguish beauty from luxury. The layout of my edition is in fact less costly than that of similar large-scale projects; Baskerville is only marginally dearer than certain somewhat tighter faces; only on a relatively minor component, the paper – specially made, and with a VOLTAIRE watermark – did I spend rather more than I need have done.

Let me now proceed from these principles and generalities to more specific details. The notes assembled at the end of each letter are arranged under four headings: Manuscripts, Editions, Textual notes, and Commentary, so that the reader can go directly to the category of note in which he is interested, and pass over those to which, for the moment, he is indifferent.

Under the heading Manuscripts all available information is given about the written texts of the letter. That is, the nature and status of every text is described, its whereabouts specified, and its past history traced through the salerooms and the booksellers' catalogues. In describing the manuscripts the term "holograph" is applied to a letter in the writing of its author, and "original" to one in the hand of a secretary. Such terms as draft, file copy, and the like are self-evident. "Photocopy" (though no longer correct in every case since the invention of electronic techniques) is used as a generic term to include every kind of photographic or other facsimile reproduction. I have examined nearly all the manuscripts even when they have been photographed, and I strongly recommend all scholars to do likewise. Many skipped pages, and a great variety of mistakes, expected and unexpected, were revealed by collation.

Under the heading Editions are recorded the first appearance in print, if any, of each text, and every subsequent printing of textual or editorial importance.

Textual notes were kept to a minimum when a primary manuscript was available. It was of course indispensable to give an accurate text, and to present all variants necessary for a proper understanding of the particular letter and the circumstances surrounding it. But it was out of the question to indulge in the full efflorescence of annotation which could so easily have blossomed. Many Voltaire letters have survived in several and even fifteen or twenty texts, all having more or less validity. The clearly significant texts are in themselves numerous. There are cases in which we have a draft; the actual letter sent to the correspondent; a copy or several copies sent by Voltaire to others for their information, nearly always with modifications; the text as edited by Voltaire for publication at the time, and perhaps again and differently for subsequent publications; copies made by the recipient and other contemporaries, and by them modified for specific purposes. All such variants are of course potentially important as giving clues to Voltaire's thinking and to his relations with persons and events, and therefore they have been scrupulously noted. Fortunately, letters in which all these kinds of variants occur are relatively few. Of course the operative word here is "relatively," for in a correspondence of 20,000 letters almost anything can and does occur absolutely often, even if relatively seldom.

11031

Voltaire to Elie Bertrand

aux Délices 15e May 1764

Iliacos intra muros peccatur et extra[1].

Mais, mon cher philosophe, Berne aura la gloire de tout pacifier, il lui suffira de dire *Quos ego*[2]? On ne connait pas trop icy les fadaises de Guillaume Vadé; ce sont des joujous faits pour amuser des Français, et dont les têtes solides de la Suisse ne s'accommoderaient guères. Cependant, s'il y a icy quelques éxemplaires je ne manquerai pas de vous en faire avoir un. J'aimerais bien mieux être chargé par l'Electeur Palatin de vous présenter quelque chose de plus éssentiel.

Je vous suis infiniment obligé de la bonté que vous avez eue de m'envoier les irrigations[3]. Je vous supplie de présenter mes très humbles remerciements à Monsieur vôtre frère; nous lui devrons, mes vaches et moi de grandes actions de grâce. Nous ne sommes pas, dans nôtre paϊs de Gex de si bons cultivateurs que les Bernois, mais je fais ce que je peux pour les imiter, et je crois rendre service à mon prochain quand je fais croitre quatre brins d'herbe sur un terrein qui n'en portait que deux[4]. J'ai bâti des maisons, planté des arbres, marié des filles, l'ange exterminateur n'a rien à me dire, et je passerai hardiment sur le pont aigu[5]. En attendant, je vous aimerai bien véritablement mon cher philosophe, tant que je vègéterai dans ce monde.

[*address:*] à Monsieur / Monsieur Bertrand 1er Pasteur de l'église / française, membre de plusieurs académies et[a] / à Berne /

MANUSCRIPTS

1. original (Archiwum akt dawnych, Warsaw, Zbiór Anny Branickiej, in MS.236; photocopy Th. B).

EDITIONS

1. first printed in the *Lettres inédites de Voltaire* (Paris 1818), pp.139-140.

COMMENTARY

On the same day, Crommelin wrote to Lullin from Paris: 'J'écrivis l'autre jour un petit billet à Mr de Montigny, pour lui demander réponse au petit Mémoire que je lui avois remis pour le changement à faire du chemin pour le port du sel dans les enclaves, et pour qu'il

Then there are various kinds of later transcripts, including those made by editors for publication. Among these only one series is of real importance – the copies made for the Kehl edition. I acquired these 2,790 transcripts from the Beaumarchais family, not without various difficulties, and found them of great interest. They are faithful secretarial copies, but their chief importance lies in the fact that they show the editorial work, much of it positively hair-raising, done on them by the Kehl editors. They also bear a number of manuscript notes by Condorcet, Beaumarchais, and Decroix.

Even in the primary manuscripts by no means all the variants are always important, and therefore only those which are significant have been recorded. When we turn to the secondary manuscripts and to the printed texts, hardly any discrepancies have value. In particular, I deprecate the practice of recording mistakes by previous editors for the sole purpose of pointing them out. As a rule this is mere showing-off, and serves no useful purpose. Besides, apart from this general principle, the inaccuracies in the published Voltaire texts are extremely numerous. If the proliferation of punctuation, capitalization, and the like be included, they run to hundreds of thousands.

It is all too easy for an editor to decry the efforts of his predecessors and to judge their often extravagant procedures by the standards of his own generation. Yet in fairness it must be said that Voltaire's correspondence (with the exception of a few small collections) had never before been edited at all in any scholarly sense of the word. The Kehl edition of 1785–1789 is the only compilation based on the manuscripts, and even in that edition many of Voltaire's letters were printed with a somewhat modified regard for what he actually wrote. Since then the text has undergone the vagaries of taste and censorship resulting from wars, revolutions, restorations, and the mere efflux of time. Each generation of editors has left its mark on it; and as each one has been content in the main to follow the immediately preceding editions, the changes have cumulated. In the event, I found that the standard Moland text of 1880–1882 does not contain a single letter printed completely accurately, while half of it contains substantial defects of every imaginable kind. This is not surprising since Moland ignored the thousands of manuscripts available to him even in Paris, where he worked. Again, it would clearly be little more than learned exhibitionism to point out these mistakes unless they have some particular interest.

The texts have of course been presented, for the first time, without suppression, multilation, or addition of any kind. All known letters by and to Voltaire are printed in full. The same rule applies to the correspondence of mme Du Châtelet (except for most of her loveletters to Saint-Lambert), and to that of mme Denis during Voltaire's lifetime – these two series forming integral parts of Voltaire's correspondence. Some letters exchanged between third persons concerning Voltaire have also been included, especially in the early years; in these, irrelevant passages, duly indicated, have sometimes been omitted. Lost letters about which definite information is available are recorded as briefly as possible: but this has been done, with few exceptions, only for those written by Voltaire himself. Even so I must say that this practice has been useful in bringing quite a number of buried letters to the surface. All letters are set out in a single chronological sequence.

Only true letters have been included. There are necessarily a few doubtful cases, but dedications and literary works in epistolary form have been excluded. So have epistles in verse; but this presents a difficult problem, for many of the compositions now classed with Voltaire's poetry originally formed parts of letters; again, Voltaire sometimes wrote letters entirely in verse, and so did some of his correspondents. Each case was therefore decided on its merits. On the other hand, numerous and often very important documents have been printed in the appendixes, nearly all for the first time.

Only the physical presentation of the texts has been slightly modified, in the sense that letters reproduced from secondary sources have been modernized; but these are relatively few in number. The vast majority of the letters has been printed from manuscripts, and these have been reproduced faithfully, but not slavishly (as have a few literal transcripts). In fact it is seldom useful to reproduce French eighteenth-century manuscripts *literatim*, for the French language was by then frozen and has hardly been modified since. But in the case of Voltaire it is interesting to reproduce his spelling, because he was a conscious reformer and innovator, though it would be a futile anachronism to do so in a palaeographic spirit. I had already edited *Voltaire's notebooks* in such a spirit, and then realized that the resulting text was quite difficult to read, without having any compensating advantages.

One need only point out that Voltaire hardly ever used an apostrophe: he wrote *jose* for *j'ose* and *mont* for *m'ont*. His use of capital letters is almost totally erratic: he seldom wrote one even after a full stop, and such forms as *paris* and *dalembert* very often fall from his pen. He usually made no distinction between *u* and *v*, *i* and *j*. All these details have been normalized, except in a few cases, in particular the letters of mme Du Châtelet, where it seemed useful to preserve the full flavour of texts written in a pre-eighteenth-century manner. The use of the long *ʃ* has not been followed. When Voltaire used an accent it has been reproduced even if it now looks wrong, and when he omitted one it has been supplied. However, I have distinguished, so far as possible, between deliberately written accents, and those which fell indifferently from Voltaire's quill. Thus, when he placed a dot instead of a *circonflexe* over an *i*, or the other way about, it was deliberate; but when he freely interchanged grave and acute accents, this was no more significant then than it is now, since everyone who writes any accented language rapidly does the same thing.

The spelling of all proper names, foreign words, and quotations has been reproduced as it stands, whatever the source.

Voltaire's punctuation is important for the rhythm of his

sentences, and even for his grammar and meaning; but here again some measure of editorial discretion is required, for eighteenth-century writers were disconcertingly casual in this respect. For instance, when Voltaire wrote a semi-colon after a question, it would be absurd not to replace it by a question-mark. Difficulty is often caused by the comma and the full stop, which Voltaire regarded as almost interchangeable. In such cases, I have introduced a minimum of regularity, without attempting to modernize. Punctuation is often lacking entirely, and there I have added it, but only to the extent indispensable for understanding the text.

In addition, Voltaire's manuscripts present editorial problems peculiar to him, and this is, in part, the result of the extent and duration of his correspondence. It is not to be expected that a man, even a French eighteenth-century writer with deeply ingrained classical convictions, should write for seventy years without some changes appearing in his use of language. And, as I mentioned earlier, he made some deliberate reforms. Thus, in the *Siècle de Louis XIV*, Voltaire introduced the spelling of *ai* for *oi* wherever the diphthong was so pronounced. In his time *français*, for instance, though pronounced as it is today, was still written *françois*. And Voltaire suppressed practically all capital letters, an attempted reform in which he did not persist, but which left its mark on his subsequent manuscripts. I may perhaps be allowed to add that I have myself tried to put into practice some of Voltaire's less extreme ideas about the use of capital letters.

Voltaire's familiar letters, even some of the most elegant, were often dashed off at great speed, and contain apparent mistakes in grammar and spelling, in addition to the usual ones concerning the commonest French accents. Needless to say, nothing of this kind has been "corrected." It would have been intolerable to do so if one could, and in any case who is to say in every case what is intended and what is a slip of the pen? Moreover, not only have I not corrected such "mistakes," I have not even drawn attention to them by scattering *sic*s all over Voltaire's manuscripts. I feel, indeed, that the intrusive editorial *sic* is very much overdone. A scholarly editor implicitly undertakes to produce a correct text in accordance with the norms he has laid down. Whenever he then adds a *sic* he is in effect saying to the reader: "I presume that you have no confidence in me and I therefore assure you that I have not made a mistake." This does not strike me as a very elegant posture.

All or very nearly all the manuscripts have been photocopied in, or transformed into, directly legible form, and these photocopies have been bound to form a permanent record at the Institut Voltaire, so that any scholar who wishes to check the accuracy of my texts or to make more minutely literal transcripts can easily do so. This set of photocopies so far extends to over 160 substantial volumes, and is not yet completely bound. Whenever the original reproduction was on microfilm, that also has been preserved and carefully inventoried.

The decisions to be taken concerning the other kind of annotation, that forming what I have called the Commentary, were even more complex. One rule was easy to make, for I have always had strong views on the annotation of such publications as this. I believe it to be unnecessary and even absurd to tell the reader everything, over and over again, in every publication. I shall name no names, but examples will no doubt occur to you. What is the use of having dictionaries of biography, of languages, of geography, of every field of knowledge, if whenever a name or an event is mentioned, or an unusual word occurs, a footnote is provided which simply summarizes the evidence given even in books as well known and accessible as the *Dictionary of national biography* and the *Oxford English dictionary*? I think, indeed I am sure, that the purpose of biographical annotation in any extensive scholarly work should be to identify the person mentioned if this is not immediately evident, and no more. More detailed information should be given only when it is not available in standard works of reference. Thus, I have devoted a great deal of research to the identification of obscure people, very often, indeed, searching through archival and other manuscript sources, but have not thought it necessary to give any general information about the personages and events recorded in every encyclopaedia.

In the same way, I do not see what useful purpose is served by pointing out that a particular form or meaning or spelling does not correspond to today's usage. After all, this is obvious to every reader. What is important is to distinguish a genuine variant from a slip of the pen, and above all to point out forms and usages different from or earlier than those recorded in the standard dictionaries.

This problem of annotation is aggravated in the case of Voltaire's correspondence by two special factors. One of these is Voltaire's universality, which makes him of interest to almost all scholars: and thus it cannot be assumed that the same basic information is possessed by all. Those who want to look up Voltaire's views on the regeneration of snails, Latin prosody, the historicity of Abraham, the increase in weight of calcified metal, or the virginity of Joan of Arc, do not necessarily have the same background of knowledge, and allowance had to be made for this fact. The other special factor is the international character of the project itself: an Englishman working in Switzerland on a Frenchman. This fact caused some awkward difficulties, which had also to be taken into account, like those connected with the all-embracing nature of Voltaire's interests.

I have spoken of certain types of annotation which in my opinion should be restricted, and which, for good or ill, had to be so restricted on this occasion. On the other hand, there is one kind of note to which I have attached great importance, much more so than in many other scholarly works. I refer to the identification of books, periodicals, and other publications. It can be extremely important to know exactly which text or edition Voltaire used, and I have gone to a great deal of trouble to give this information as fully and as accurately as possible. As a result, I may be allowed to say that the list of works cited in my footnotes constitutes a modest contribution to eighteenth century bibliography. And it has also been possible to clarify a good many difficulties connected with the infinitely complex bibliography of Voltaire's own writings.

The first major editorial problem to be resolved was simple in essence and infinitely difficult in execution: the location of the manuscripts. In none of the existing editions, except a very few specialized ones like the admirable volume of Lucien Foulet, whom I had the privilege of knowing in his old age, was the whereabouts of the manuscript sources specified even when, exceptionally, they were used. There are even one or two so-called scholars alive today who not only abstain from indicating their sources, but positively refuse to name them even when they are asked for them privately. I have made a point of indicating in my notes whenever a modern editor has failed to specify the location of his manuscript sources. In the case of Voltaire the task of finding the manuscripts was a singularly difficult one, since he had over 1,700 correspondents throughout the western world. Moreover, he acquired a wide reputation when young, and his letters were so much admired that they were collected and published even during his life-time, to his great annoyance. This means that the manuscripts were always widely dispersed, and are now to be found everywhere and anywhere, from Helsinki to Honolulu.

There were also special problems, such as those presented by German archives and libraries, even the known contents of which were sometimes lost during and after the second world war, or removed to some other depository in the west or east, or simply stolen, like Frederick's letters to Voltaire, which are still slowly emerging from their hiding place. Fortunately, nearly all the manuscripts at first reported as destroyed in French libraries have since turned up safe and sound, many unfortunately too late for the edition. There were also the usual difficulties resulting from the very varying notions possessed by custodians of papers about their responsibilities to scholars. Gresham's law has begun to operate even in this country, and American libraries are showing signs of becoming infected by the practices prevalent in certain European countries. But this is exceptional. In general I cannot praise too highly the facilities provided by so many custodians in numerous countries.

There was also a commercial problem. Because so many manuscripts have survived, single Voltaire letters, and even whole series of them, still appear in sales and in dealers' catalogues. Once they are sold they are difficult to trace, and so I have been obliged to buy a very large number, at rapidly increasing prices. Most of them I have presented to the Institut Voltaire, together with its library and some of the contents of its museum. Incidentally, one of the finest collections of Voltaire manuscripts is now to be found in the new world, at the Pierpont Morgan library.

I should like to acknowledge also the enlightened attitude of many dealers. Only once have I encountered an obscurantist attitude. This was when a New York dealer called Kraus acquired a large collection of letters, some of which contain references to Voltaire. These have long since been published, but even so this dealer refuses to allow me to collate them.

I cannot deny that all sorts of difficulties were experienced, but in the end patience and persistence overcame nearly all of them. I finally succeeded in locating the manuscripts of about 95 per cent of the then known letters, as well as the manuscripts of about 10,000 letters not in the standard edition – though this involved me in a correspondence nearly as extensive as Voltaire's. These figures are true today, but unfortunately they do not fully apply to the actual edition, for many of the manuscripts, including those of a thousand more unpublished letters, have turned up during the course of its publication, and indeed in part by virtue of the publication.

I have passed over many other problems common to all such editions, but there are two I may be forgiven for mentioning in conclusion. I refer to the identification of the correspondents and the dating of the letters. So far as the former difficulty is concerned, I will say only this: in the vast mass of his correspondence the addressees of only a hundred letters written by Voltaire remained unidentified, and a few of these puzzles have since been solved.

The dating was not established quite as satisfactorily as that, but the difficulties were much greater, for Voltaire hardly ever dated a letter in full. Allow me to illustrate this difficulty from a series of letters which I had the great good fortune to discover a few years ago, unfortunately too late for the edition – Voltaire's early loveletters to his niece. Of the 142 unpublished letters in this series only three are completely dated (one by a secretary) and twenty-three partially so. To make matters worse mme Denis later endorsed dates on the manuscripts, dates which are usually wrong, and the more circumstantial they are the more inaccurate they tend to be. Thus she wrote "2 septembre 1743" on a letter which, from internal evidence, was written in February 1742. Another, dated by her "12 octobre 1745" was in fact sent on 7 December 1747. After such pedantic mistakes one is relieved to find merely a 1738 for 1748.

I did manage to date all the letters in *Voltaire's correspondence*, but in a number of cases only approximately, and some mistakes have since been revealed by the discovery of new texts or more information. On the whole, however, I am not too displeased with the result, and I have even tasted from time to time the modest joy of one who makes an inspired guess. Thus, when many of mme Du Châtelet's letters to comte d'Argental turned up in the saleroom after I had reprinted them in *Voltaire's correspondence*, I found that five of these letters bore dates which had been suppressed by the original editor. I had dated the first of these letters *circa* 25 December 1736, and the correct date was 27 December; for the second I had suggested *circa* 3 January 1737, whereas the true date was 2 January; the third I had dated "?22 January 1737," and the query turned out to be superfluous; the fourth I had correctly placed at 25 January 1737; with the fifth I was not quite so lucky, for instead of 28 January 1737 I had proposed 1/2 February.

I hope that I will be forgiven for the inevitably personal tone of this paper.

Letters and Journals of Fanny Burney: Establishing the Text

JOYCE HEMLOW

THE MANUSCRIPTS OF the letters and journals of Fanny Burney – Madame d'Arblay – which with the changes in ownership were inaccessible for 100 years, have been made available to scholars since the late 1940s in the Henry W. and Albert A. Berg Collection of the New York Public Library, while the complement to this material reached the British Museum with the acquisition of "The Barrett Collection of Burney Papers" in 1952.[1] Sent as actual copy to the press in 1842–1847, the manuscripts of the so-called *Diary and Letters* carry on their surfaces three layers of editorial markings and changes. To penetrate to the original text, one must first understand how, why, and in what order the modifications were introduced. The history of the previous editings follows in some respects the provenance of the Burney papers.

The Burney manuscripts, of which Madame d'Arblay's letters and journals form a part, may be defined, for the purposes of this

1 / See C. E. Wright, *The British Museum Quarterly*, XVIII (1953), 41–43; John D. Gordan, "A Doctor's Benefaction: The Berg Collection of the New York Public Library," *The Papers of the Bibliographical Society of America*, XLVIII (1954), 308–11; and Joyce Hemlow, intro., *A Catalogue of the Burney Family Correspondence 1749–1878* (1968).

paper, as the writings of Charles Burney (1726–1814), Mus. Doc. (1769), and his family of eight (surviving) children, six by a first marriage and two by a second. The first family included Esther (1749–1832), an accomplished harpsichordist; James (1750–1821), rear-admiral (1821); Frances (1752–1840), journalist and novelist; Susannah Elizabeth (1755–1800), later Mrs. Molesworth Phillips; Charles Jr. (1757–1817), D.D. (1812), schoolmaster, Greek scholar, and divine; and Charlotte Ann (1761–1838), who became the wife of Clement Francis (d. 1792) and later of Ralph Broome (d. 1805). Her daughter Charlotte (Francis) Barrett (1786–1870) was to be Madame d'Arblay's first editor. *Diary and Letters of Madame d'Arblay* (7 volumes), edited by her niece, was published (1842–47) by Henry Colburn of Great Marlborough Street.

Dr. Burney's second family comprised Richard Thomas (1768–1808), who early went to India, becoming a schoolmaster at Kidderpore; and Sarah Harriet (1772–1844), the second novelist of the family.

The letters and journals exchanged between the feminine members of the family were voluminous, trusting, frank, and calculated to provide entertainment. In the early days at St. Martin's Street, Leicester Square, the young Burneys found copy enough in the Italian singers, the travellers, literati, and actors, the artists, divines, and statesmen who accepted invitations to Dr. Burney's evening musicales; and abroad in the eighteenth-century London season there were operas, rehearsals, concerts, benefits, exhibitions, and theatre (especially Garrick in all his great rôles), to say nothing of pleasure grounds like Ranelagh Gardens or Vauxhall. In later years the Burneys so fortunate as to be in fascinating company abroad could journalize in a minute and entertaining manner for the Burneys left at home. From Chessington to the court, from Streatham (where Dr. Johnson was ensconced with his friends the Thrales) to Brussels and the Battle of Waterloo, there was copy enough if one had the knack, as Fanny Burney had, of securing a front seat at the chief events of her time. Scores of such journals, the bulky accumulations of almost forty years, with the "alives" or short family letters reporting on health and the like, were to be augmented in time with the letters of the third, and eventually, the fourth, generation of Burneys. Some of these last, growing up in the nineteenth century, were involved in evangelical movements within the church; others, venturing further afield, wrote accounts of their travels in France, Italy, or India.

The scope of interest, the range of friendships (from the humblest to most exalted in the land), the literary, professional, and social activities of the Burney family, are reflected in an extant correspondence of some 10,000 items now listed, in large part at least, in *A Catalogue of the Burney Family Correspondence 1748–1878* (1968) compiled by the writer with the assistance of Jeanne M. Burgess and Althea Douglas. Included is an index (of about 1,000 correspondents) and an introduction which gives the provenance of large sections or blocks of the papers as they were inherited by different branches of the family.

As the papers descended through the branches of the family they met differing fates. Some sections of the original correspondence, known from references in other letters to have existed, seemingly exist no longer, having in all probability been burned. Some sections were hoarded and later sold; some were reserved or given away as nuclei for autograph collections. And some, falling into strong editorial hands, were destroyed in part, mutilated in part, ruthlessly excised, or covered in part with obliterating ink. Into this latter category fell the papers of Fanny Burney and with them Dr. Burney's correspondence and memoirs.

It was the custom in the eighteenth and nineteenth centuries, at the deaths of the *recipients*, to return packets of letters received, usually docketed and suitably tied, to the *writers*. The letter was the property of the writer and was often so claimed.

And thus it was that through successive deaths in the Burney and d'Arblay families, the massive journals that Fanny Burney had written to her sister Susan (d. 1800), her letters to other sisters, to her father, brothers, husband, and son (d. 1837), were eventually returned to her. And since Dr. Burney before his death in 1814 had chosen her for his editor, his papers also went to her.

Always mindful that many of the records might be of interest to future ages, but by no means unmindful of the memory of her father and the honour of the family, she began in the summer of 1817 at Ilfracombe to read her father's letters and memoirs and to make selections for possible publication. It was not, however, until 1819–20 when – after the death of her husband, General d'Arblay, in 1818 – she returned to London, establishing a home for her son at 11 Bolton Street, Piccadilly, that she began the editorial work that was to occupy her for the next twenty years. On 13 June 1820 she would have been 68 years old, and the dark editorial ink that she used as a favour to her eyes lies starkly over the older paler ink of her original writing. Her editorial procedures, further, were characteristic, consistent, and easily distinguishable from the work of the editors who were to follow her.

Generally speaking, she had in her own hoards three classes of material to edit. There were compositions like the journals of Ilfracombe, Dunkirk, Trèves, or Waterloo, which were written five or six or more years after the events described, by recourse to memory, memoranda taken at the time, and contemporary letters written or received. Written at one of the dying or farewell requests of the general and designed for reading at her son's "rectory fireside" to the dream grandchildren who, though she did not know it, were never to be born, these compositions needed in her view little revising and they can be edited today as semi-literary works.

In the second place there were compositions like the court journals, more accurately described perhaps as monthly chronicles. But they were written for and sent to one person (namely,

Mrs. Phillips) as letters were written and sent, although by cart or coach because of their weight, and so they may be called journal-letters. Composed in thick packets covering a month at a time, sometimes dispatched at the end of the month in question, but sometimes written months later by the aid of memory and memoranda, these journals too, though sent to Mrs. Phillips at monthly intervals, were designed for semi-public reading – at Norbury Park, for instance. Those that Madame d'Arblay selected for publication needed in her view few suppressions or changes. Diaries, in the sense of records of the activities (whether interesting or not) of each day, it was not her practice to keep. Rather, she took down memoranda or transcripts of conversation, which she later incorporated in journals.

Quite different from the journals or journal-letters, however, were familiar letters sent to or received from members of the d'Arblay or Burney families. Following the example of her father who, after the death of his second wife in 1796, destroyed 500 or more of his letters to her, which he found she had saved, and an equal number of her replies to them (1,000 letters in all),[2] Madame d'Arblay also destroyed, as why should she not, letters of a personal or private nature. Often it was at the request of some member of the family that she destroyed records, as when her sister, Charlotte Broome, asked her to find and burn disagreeable letters relating to the late Ralph Broome Sr. (d. 1805). She needed no prompting, however, to burn letters bearing on family disgraces, difficulties, or disagreements, discreditable matter of any kind, or even material, otherwise innocuous, that might give pain or offence to surviving members of the family or to friends. Esther (Burney) Burney likewise burned the heartbroken records of Susan's sojourn in Ireland, and, as one of her father's residuary legatees, much of his correspondence. Her own, largely missing, may also have been burned by her own hand or wishes.

The letters that Madame d'Arblay allowed to survive,

2 / See Doctor Burney's "Memoirs" (Berg) and his A.L.S. (Berg) to Thomas Twining, December 6, 1796.

particularly her own to her father and his to her, she curtailed drastically. Of the double sheets, quarto, of good rag bond, on which the normal four-paged letters were written, she often tore away the second leaf, either obliterating at the bottom of the second page a sentence thus left incomplete; or, alternately, completing the sentence by re-writing on the lower margin of the second page the matter originally at the top of page three. Often she tore away a first leaf, sometimes camouflaging the second as the beginning of the letter. Of the remaining pages of writing she often obliterated words, lines, sentences, paragraphs, even pages. Monetary matters, circumstances painful to the memory, harmful to the dead, or potential of pain or resentment, she obliterated with a heavily inked series of interlocking *o*'s or *e*'s. Trivia, or what she considered trivia, such as shopping or details of dress, she customarily obliterated. For instance, the "wear" she felt she needed at news of the execution of Louis XVI: "Please send my round black Gown, & my new black Linnen, & some black ribbon. ... I am ashamed not to be in black before all these deep Mourners." Or again the soap, candles, and wine that cluttered the chaise on a journey from London to Bookham in November 1796. On one occasion she over-wrote such items in pale ink with heavy black ink, omitting the soaps and improving the syntax.

Taking for granted that it is the business of a modern editor to restore the text as it was originally written, we have expended great effort to read the text obscured by the heavily inked obliterating marks. Infra-red photography has not so far been helpful, but most of the obliterated passages can be read with time, concentration, patience, magnifying devices, and strong lights. A magnifying glass made in Germany and fitted with a small but strong electric lightbulb, hooded over to shield the eyes, has been our best aid when working with the actual manuscripts. Sunlight on positive photostats will sometimes help to separate the underlying hieroglyphics from the thick overlying tracery. The magnification provided when microfilms of the obliterated manuscripts are projected on the screen of the microfilm reader is often the only assistance needed. Tracings taken of the enlarged and visible parts of the letters of a word as they are thrown on the screen provide the length, shape, and contour of the word and finally the word.

This is slow work, taking at best twenty minutes per line, at worst three or more hours per half line, but by the grace of the gods of editors, the gestalt powers of the brain, and a knowledge of Fanny Burney's idiom, the original tracings will form themselves into meaningful patterns.

Occasionally when the text suggested some sentiment that Madame d'Arblay wished she had made, she scrupled not to insert it interlinearly. Better late than never, even if the sentiment may not have been an accurate reflection of her mood of twenty or thirty years ago. Interpolated, for instance, in her reply to a letter of 14 April 1794 from her father, in which he had described an unexpected meeting with Mrs. Thrale: "[I] wish few things more earnestly than again to meet her."

Often she dated letters from the postmarks normally appearing on the address panel on page two. The contents of the letters (or of the parts she had left unobliterated) she summarized in a caption written on the upper lefthand corner of the first page. Thus: "Babe Alex / M. de Lally / Mad de Lally / Mr. Mason / Pursuits of Literature / M^{rs}: Delany / " Indicated on the upper margin of the first page also was the status she accorded to letters with respect to their suitability for publication or other pretensions to survival.

※ meant save and possibly publish
⁜ the same, only recommended rather less
⊕ read and keep
O do not publish

Even, however, as Madame d'Arblay examined the old hoards, new letters accrued. With the death of her son, the poet-preacher Alexander d'Arblay, in January 1837 she was overwhelmed, and not by grief alone. "[My poor Alex's] MSS – his papers – who shall decypher Them? – Who but I see their various contents? – & there is a hoard immense – I owe it to him to not let *one* be investigated but by myself & I am blinded by them – & can go on but a short time – "[3] A year later as her strength and eyesight failed she was forced to relinquish the work begun a full twenty years before of examining, destroying, and editing family papers: "My eyes will work at them no more!"

But what to do with the accumulations, the hoards, the "myriads" of mss. was the question. Madame d'Arblay consulted her sister Charlotte Broome and her niece Charlotte Barrett: "My dear Charlottes BOTH – think for me ... what I had best do with this killing mass of constant recurrence to my calamity. – Shall I burn them? at once – or shall I, & can I, so [modify] a division as to spare for future times various collections that may be amusing & even instructive –[4]

The decision on the future of the Burney papers – whether they were to be burned, hoarded, edited, or printed in part – she left ultimately to her heirs. In a will made on 6 March 1839 and probated on 17 February 1840 (P.C.C. Arden, 88) she returned her father's papers to his grandson in the male line, Charles Parr Burney (1785–1864):

> to my Nephew Dr. Charles Parr Burney I leave the entire arrangement of the correspondence of my dear Father excepting my own Letters which I give to my Niece Charlotte Barrett. I had already in the last year made it over to my beloved Son who was preparing it for the press. I now commit it to Dr. Cs Burney either for a small select publication or for the flames – I leave him likewise indiscriminately & without reserve or direction whatever composition may remain in the handwriting of my dear Father whether in prose

3 / A.L.S. (Berg), [1 Apr. 1837].
4 / A.L.S. (Berg), [20 Apr. 1838].

or in verse well assured that I cannot do more honor to his memory.

the whole of my own immense Mass of MSS. collected from my 15th year whether personal or collateral consisting of letters Diaries Journals Dramas compositions in prose & verse I bequeath to the care & sole and immediate possession of my niece Charlotte Barrett with full and free permission according to her unbiased taste and judgement to keep or destroy them simply but strictly stipulating that she faithfully bequeath at her death whatsoever she has not disposed of or annihilated to her son [Richard Barrett].[5]

With these papers came also the Reverend Alexander d'Arblay's manuscripts and a curious correspondence accumulated by General d'Arblay, most of which is now in the Berg Collection (see the provenance of the papers, *Catalogue*).

Charlotte Barrett lost no time; nor did the publishers who well knew that the public had not yet forgotten Fanny Burney's early life, the people either famed or notorious (like Garrick and the Earl of Sandwich) whom she had met in her father's house; her later associations with Mrs. Thrale, Dr. Johnson, Sir Joshua Reynolds, Burke, and others. Of backstairs gossip at the court they knew she knew much – much secret matter; to say nothing of notable figures and notable events in London, Bath, Brussels, and Paris. Henry Colburn of Great Marlborough Street, the fashionable and lighthearted publisher of Evelyn's *Diary* (1818) and of Pepys's *Diary* (1825), was more than willing to publish Madame d'Arblay's "Diary."

From the mass of her own papers Madame d'Arblay had already made a selection which she had edited, according to her own lights, for possible publication. And this selection, already heavily edited and truncated, Charlotte Barrett undertook to prepare for the press. Restrictions on the material even more

5 / The transcripts were taken from Charlotte Barrett's copy (1786–1870) copy of the will (Barrett).

extensive than those imposed by Fanny, on behalf of the Burney family, were now imposed from without. On the news that the letters and journals were to be printed, numbers of Madame d'Arblay's friends and correspondents sent apprehensive notes or messages to her editor prohibiting the use or publication of their letters or names. The aged and blind Princess Sophia, whom Madame d'Arblay had often been invited to visit at Kensington Palace, hoped anxiously that none of her letters or those of her sisters (of which there are extant to this day over 300) would be exposed to the public gaze. The name of Alexander d'Arblay's fiancée had to be repressed on her brother's request. Much incensed by facts about Mrs. Delany that Madame d'Arblay had adduced in *Memoirs of Doctor Burney* (3 volumes, 1832), Lady Llanover (Mrs. Delany's great-great-grand niece) stipulated that her mother Georgiana Mary Ann (Port) Waddington, who had corresponded regularly with Madame d'Arblay since 1788, should not be mentioned by name. (Letters to Mrs. Waddington were therefore labelled in the edition: "To a Friend.") And Amelia (Locke) Angerstein, one of Madame d'Arblay's closest and most idealized friends of over fifty years' standing, fearing perhaps that some of her abundant troubles with her son John Julius III would somehow emerge, requested Charlotte Barrett to repress her name and her affairs.[6] Besides such prohibitions, of which the written records are extant in Charlotte Barrett's correspondence of the time (see *Catalogue*), there were doubtless many more transmitted orally.

All such requests, as well as Madame d'Arblay's repressions of material, Charlotte Barrett honoured, and in addition she made deletions according to her own taste and judgment. Shar-

6 / Letters from Mrs. Locke and Mrs. Angerstein *to* Madame d'Arblay would have been returned, according to custom, at the death of the latter. Missing, however, in the Burney archives are Madame d'Arblay's letters to them, which perhaps Charlotte had also been persuaded to return, having been allowed to make copies of a few for publication. This correspondence, if extant, has not been made available to the editors.

ing also in the decisions on what to print and what to suppress were Charlotte's daughter Julia (Barrett) Thomas Maitland (1804–1864) and her cousin Fanny (Phillips) Raper (1782–1860), the daughter of Susannah Elizabeth (Burney) Phillips. A little disenchanted with "aunt d'Arblay," these younger editors struck out, sometimes with quite savage (at least with large and untidy) scrawls, whole pages of matter. Cancelled, for instance, were old love affairs, long folios of Richardsonian heart-searchings, the analyses, now despairing, now hopeful, of the matrimonial intentions of the Rev. George Cambridge – dubbed by Walpole "the Infallible" – by 1842 archdeacon of Middlesex, and a great friend of the Barretts. Similar deliberations relating to the Hon. Stephen Digby, the queen's vice-chamberlain – the Mr. Fairly of the printed journals – also fell under the strokes of the younger editors. Deleted by Charlotte Barrett herself were accounts of Fanny Burney's meetings in 1791 in Bath with members of the Spenser and Devonshire families as well as the comments of the gardener at Wilton House on the conduct of the tenth Earl of Pembroke. Prudence, the fear of giving offence, and the tastes of the various editors had full play. Deleted or reduced to smaller compass were superlatives and saccharine effusions. Thus "My dearest dearest dearest Father" appears in print as "My dear Father."

Destructive to the chronology of the events recorded and the historical value of the papers was Charlotte Barrett's practice of transferring material from the date under which it was written to letters of other dates. On seeing the extensive obliterations that Madame d'Arblay had made in her letters of June 13 and 18 and July 6 and 12 (Barrett) to her father and apparently deciding that the residues of the truncated letters were not worth printing as such, she decided to salvage some of the material that had been allowed to stand by Madame d'Arblay, in her editorial capacity. Charlotte therefore made a selection of paragraphs from all four letters and, copying them on a fresh sheet, constructed a "composite," which she dated

June 18; this, sent to the press, was published as a genuine letter (*Diary and Letters*, VI, pp. 45–48). The derivations of the various parts of the composite can be seen by comparing the holograph copy (Berg Collection) in Charlotte's hand with the four original letters (Barrett) in Madame d'Arblay's hand. The first four paragraphs of the copy ("My dearest Father / How I rejoice ... letter to letter.") were derived from paragraphs 1, 2, 3, and part of 4 (pages 1–3) of a letter from Madame d'Arblay to her father, dated June 13. The next two paragraphs ("I like well the idea ... *Evelina* and *Cecilia*.") were paragraphs 2 and 3 of Madame d'Arblay's original of June 18. Paragraphs 7, part of 8, and 9 ("How grieved I am ... East Indies myself!") were paragraphs 7 and 8 of the original of July 21. The closing lines of paragraph 7 ("I will make it the best ... quivering.") came from the original of July 6. And the postscript ("P.S. – The Bambino ... set right.") came from the top margin, page 1, of the original of June 18, the letter that lent its date to the composite. As Austin Dobson had no opportunity to see the original manuscripts of the so-called *Diary and Letters*, he unknowingly reprinted numbers of such composites in his edition of the *Diary and Letters* of Madame d'Arblay (6 volumes, 1904–5), the above appearing in v, pp 263–66.

The obvious task in hand is the restoration of the four originals, difficult as it may be to read the obliterated passages. In the new editions these passages will be enclosed in double half brackets to indicate what Madame d'Arblay would herself have suppressed and where occasionally the reader may expect to find shaky readings. Where the originals are known to be extant, the copies that for one reason or another Charlotte Barrett made will not be printed. Her procedures, however, will be described in minute detail in the textual notes, which if not printed, will be reproduced by some photographic or electrostatic process and deposited in the libraries having the main holdings of Burney and d'Arblay papers.

Among editors of eighteenth-century manuscripts Charlotte

Barrett must be given the prize for her work with glue-pot and scissors. In addition to copying out paragraphs for use in the composites, she often cut out desirable segments, regardless of date or addressee and pasted them down as replacements for matter that she wished to suppress or that Madame d'Arblay had obliterated. In the interest of a full, pleasant, and harmless letter, she transferred material at will, regardless of the violence done to the chronology of events.

Sometimes she took a plain sheet of paper as a base and pasted to it a series of segments cut from one letter or from a number of letters. Matter she wished to suppress she sometimes covered with a plain sheet of paper on which as a base she could paste replacements cut from other letters or from memoranda books, if such offered innocuous padding. Sometimes there was difficulty in the fitting, as when, for instance, she wished to cover lines written on a quarto page with lines written on an octavo page. All editorial problems admit of solution, however, and her practice here was to cut line-wide strips and string them end-to-end over the lines of writing beneath, her patience extending on one occasion to thirty or more such cut-outs. Less damage was done to chronology if, as sometimes happened, the discarded second leaf of a letter offered a few paste-overs for the first leaf. Sometimes, however, the transferring of sections of text did great violence to historical fact, as when, seeing an interesting account of a bread riot in Dorking that Madame d'Arblay had reported on the top margin, page 1, of her letter of 22 March 1800, she made a copy of the report and pasted it over an obliterated passage in a letter of 18 November 1800, thus changing the date of the riots by eight months.

For a final example of the changes wrought by scissors and paste, the journal-letter of May 1792 may suffice. Originally written on twelve double sheets quarto (forty-eight manuscript pages of writing in all), it was sent to the press with only twenty-two quarto pages in view. This contraction and suppression Charlotte Barrett had effected by separating the conjugate leaves of five of the double sheets, discarding some of them, and from others (as well as from three of the double sheets) cutting segments to be used as paste-ons for paragraphs she wished to suppress. The remainders of the sheets, however, from which pasteovers were cut, she luckily preserved. When the pasteovers were lifted and the discarded sheets and segments assembled, the journal was found to be substantially extant, though changed by the scissors in physical form to four double sheets, three mutilated double sheets, two single sheets, and thirty segments of various sizes (of which nineteen had been used as pasteovers). When segments and leaves were returned to their original positions it was found possible to restore forty-four of the original pages (except for two irregular segments each bearing less than a line of text). Only the second double sheet, most of which has been printed, is yet to be found.[7]

Besides the letters bearing pasteovers in the Burney Papers, there are the mutilated letters from which the pasteovers were cut. The task of the modern editor is again obvious. The paste-ons must be lifted from the letters on which they were pasted and returned to the letters from which they were cut, thus freeing the first and restoring the second. Too much praise cannot be given to the librarians of the Berg Collection of the New York Public Library and to the technicians of the photographic departments of the library for the care with which the first of these operations was carried out. To preserve for the record the state in which the *Diary and Letters* were acquired by the library, photostats were taken of the pages with their pasteovers in the position in which Charlotte Barrett had placed them. This photostat will of course give the recto of the pasteover. The pasteover was then steamed free, lifted, and its verso photographed (but photographed, as further security for the record, on the page on which it had been pasted), the same photograph showing the bared (or original) page.

7 / It could be recognized from its text: May 2. – The following week I again went to Westminster Hall ... it gratified me highly.

The pasteovers had now to be returned to the letters from which they were cut thus restoring the text of the mutilated letter. Since the mutilated letter, usually discarded for the purpose of publication, made no part of the manuscripts of the so-called *Diary and Letters*, it was likely to be found in the Barrett collection of Burney Papers in the British Museum. That is to say, the pasteover and its sources were separated by the ocean. By this time, however, there were, in the Burney Room at McGill University, catalogue cards for each manuscript letter and for each stray segment with measured descriptions of both fragments and mutilated letters. There were, besides, microfilms or photostats of all of Madame d'Arblay's journals and letters that we knew to be extant. For the first time it was possible to examine Berg and Barrett material simultaneously and so compare the shape and size of a segment lifted from a Berg manuscript with a lacuna observed in a mutilated Barrett manuscript in the British Museum or *vice versa*. Though the catalogue helped, the credit for the restoration of the pieces of manuscript to their original locations must go to Althea Douglas, who with a memory for shapes, sizes, forms, and a general acquaintance with the text as a whole, succeeded in fitting the pieces recto and verso into their original positions, thus restoring the text from which they were taken. The fitting could moreover be verified. With the excision of a section of the text wanted, for example, on the recto of a page, the scissors cut horizontally through lines of writing on the verso, separating lines and words into upper and lower halves. With the restoration of the recto these words on the verso hooked up, even if the *i* might be in New York and its dot in London, a sentence in the British Museum and the period closing it in the New York Public Library. The pieces, it might be said, fitted to a *t*, the *t* on one side of the Atlantic, its cross on the other.

Into the text of the new edition these pieces will be fitted silently with no seams showing. Only the textual notes will tell the tale of the excised segments, their sojourn on alien letters, and their return, if not physically, as an ocean still rolls between, yet nonetheless in the mind, in the transcripts, and in the new edition of the letters. Stray segments, the source of which cannot now be found, will be printed as such. One day the remainder may turn up.

Of what was left it was Charlotte's aim to make a smoothly running unexceptionable text such as could be safely read *en famille* in a quiet rectory. Starker terms in common use in the eighteenth century were therefore emended:

Good God, Susy *to* Indeed, Susy
leg *to* limb
bloody *to* sanguinary
devilish rotten boroughs *to* rotten boroughs

Slight emendation in longer passages could easily, however, change the point of view and the drive or thrust of the original writing. Madame d'Arblay by no means approved, it seems clear, the spoliation of the dead at the Battle of Waterloo.

In one place, we were entirely stopt, by a group that had gathered round a Horse, of which a British Soldier was examining one of the knees. The Animal was a tall War Horse, & one of the noblest of his species, in Shape, size, colour & carriage. These are not, I know, Horse terms; but I have no Horse Dictionary; & I have still less its contents by rote. The soldier was enumerating to his hearers its high qualities, & exultingly acquainting them it was his own property, as he had taken it, if I understood him right, from the Field, from the side of his Master, who had fallen from him, shot dead. He produced also a very fine Ring, which was all he had taken of spoil, leaving the rest to others, while he secured the Horse, which he had walked gently to Brussels.

Yet this Man gravely added, that pillage had been forbidden by the Commander in Chief! & thought that those who took the purse, Watch, &c, would have to refund! – (Diary mss. [6389]–90, Berg)

Shades, flavours, immediacy, are lost in the revision:

> In one place we were entirely stopped by a group that had gathered round a horse, of which a British soldier was examining one of the knees. The animal was a tall war-horse, and one of the noblest of his species. The soldier was enumerating to his hearers its high qualities, and exultingly acquainting them it was his own property, as he had taken it, if I understood right, from the field. He produced also a very fine ring, which was all he had taken of spoil. Yet this man gravely added that pillage had been forbidden by the Commander-in-Chief! (*Diary*, v. 171)

At the top of the first pages of the letters and covering the summaries of contents that Madame d'Arblay in her editorial capacity had written on the top left margins of the first page, Charlotte Barrett pasted tabs of paper (usually 1.2″ × 3″) on which she wrote the addresses of the letters to be printed, for example, "To Doctor Burney." With this final paste-on Charlotte seemed to think the letter ready to send to press. And the actual letters sent thus as printer's copy had to be repurchased from the publishers later, as Charlotte's correspondence with Henry Foss (*Catalogue*) indicates.

At the press, especially as the number of volumes had reached five or six with much yet to print, there were again editorial directions to delete. Colburn thought he could well dispense with six octavo pages of circuitous circumstances leading up to Madame d'Arblay's presentation to the Duchess of Angoulême: "NB. Better omit all this fruitless attempt to wait on the Duchess. She *was* presented afterwards & relates it at length." "Omit," in red ink, was often the final decision on letters with texts already much deleted.

There were pencilled directions for paragraphing as Colburn put one of his staff to work on the text, and at least one editor with a sharpened stylistic sense went meticuliously over the sentences introducing improvements in syntax. These changes also are listed in detail in the textual notes.

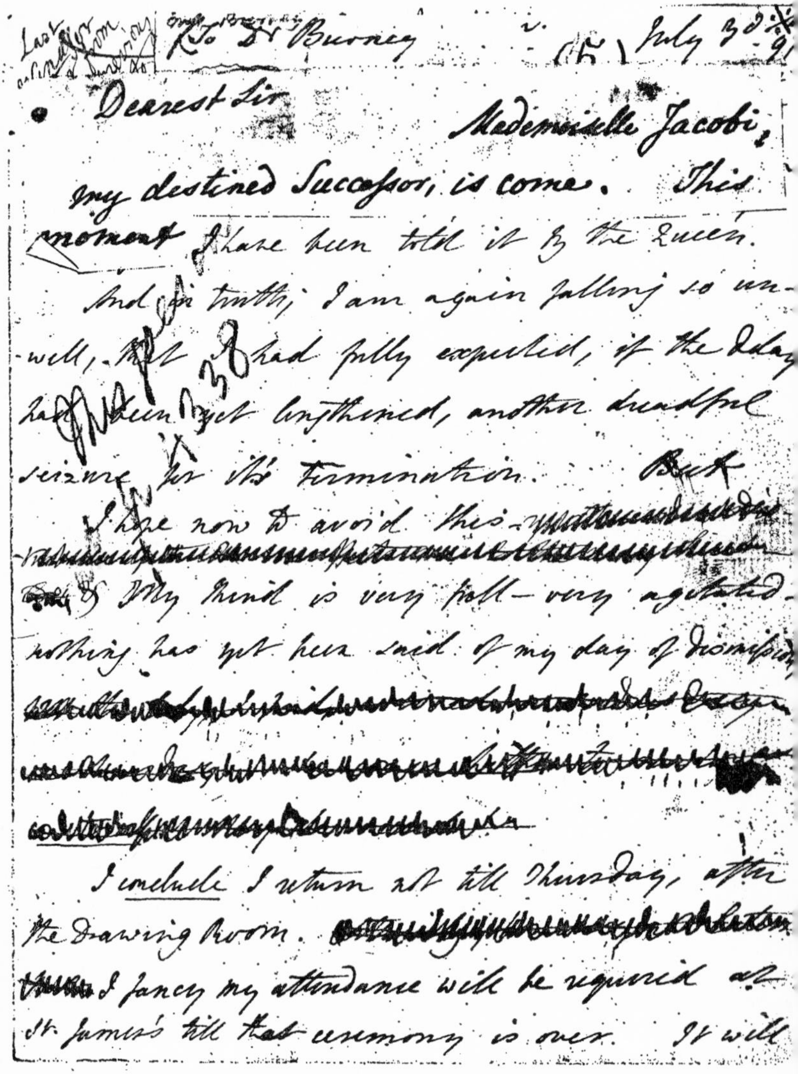

To Dr Burney July 30 — 91

Dearest Sir

Mademoiselle Jacobi, my destined Successor, is come. This moment I have been told it by the Queen.

And in truth, I am again falling so unwell, that I had fully expected, if the delay had been yet lengthened, another dreadful seizure for its termination. But

I hope now to avoid this — [illegible]

My mind is very full — very agitated — nothing has yet been said of my day of dismission [illegible]

I conclude I return not till Thursday, after the Drawing Room. [illegible] I fancy my attendance will be required at St. James's till that ceremony is over. It will

A letter (in the Berg Collection, NYPL) from Fanny Burney to her fathe Dr. Burney, showing her editorial work of later years, that of her niece, Charlot Barrett, and directions by the Press.

The text, the present editors suggest, should be as close to Fanny Burney's original writing as print can make it. Orthographical peculiarities, such as abnormally large *S*s, *K*s, and *M*s will be printed in lower case, but the eighteenth-century capitalization (used for emphasis), and the normal eighteenth-century abbreviations will be kept. A bibliographical note will give the location of the letter, its date, physical proportions, postmarks, address, and as a guide to the textual notes, an indication of whether or not it had been edited, and by whom.[8]

8 / For hints on the procedures to be followed once the text is established, this editor wishes to acknowledge a debt to previous papers published by the Editorial Conference Committee of the University of Toronto, and to thank them for an invitation to the most informative and helpful Conference of 1967.

William Blake's Protean Text

G.E. BENTLEY, JR.

THE ESTABLISHMENT OF Blake's text[1] is my problem today, as it has been for the last five or six years. When the Clarendon Press asked me to undertake an edition of his writings, I had a fairly extensive acquaintance with works by and about him. I was confident that I knew the chief problems and how to go about finding solutions for them. I believed that the right approach followed vigorously would bring satisfactory answers. As I say, I was five years younger then. I am still confident that the methods are appropriate, but I am no longer sure that satisfactory answers are possible. A scholar's job is to define as

1 / Blake's works have been edited by D. G. Rossetti, A. Gilchrist, *Life of William Blake, "Pictor Ignotus"* (1863), II; W. M. Rossetti, *The Poetical Works of William Blake* (1874); E. J. Ellis and W. B. Yeats, *The Works of William Blake* (1893), III; and largely established by John Sampson, *The Poetical Works of William Blake* (1905); Sir Geoffrey Keynes, *The Writings of William Blake* (1925) and many other works, culminating in *The Complete Writings of William Blake* (1966); D. J. Sloss and J. P. R. Wallis, *The Prophetic Writings of William Blake* (1926); and D. V. Erdman, *The Poetry and Prose of William Blake* (1966). Of course, I can only hope to refine the work of my predecessors, largely through more thorough bibliographical annotation and more consistent reference to the integral designs.

narrowly as possible the limits of uncertainty. I may be no more certain of the answers than others are – indeed, I believe I am often less certain – but I am fairly clear about the limits of probability. I am considerably better supplied with problems than with solutions. Blake's text exhibits all the changes of Proteus. One of his editor's most important tasks is to determine where, or whether, the true Blake is behind the changes.

Two facts largely determine the information available to an editor of Blake's writings. The first is his remarkable personal obscurity. What little fame he had was as a designer and vision-seer. Only three of his works were quoted by the British press during his lifetime, and of one poem the reviewer said: "Should he again essay to climb the Parnassian heights, his friends would do well to restrain his wanderings with the strait waistcoat. Whatever license we may allow him as a painter, to tolerate him as a poet would be insufferable."[2] As a consequence, we can expect very little external help from magazines or letters of Blake's friends in dating his works, in analysing their mode of publication, or in understanding the effect they made upon his contemporaries. What evidence there is is almost entirely internal.

The second determining fact is the form in which Blake's writings survive. Blake wrote voluminously, and a friend reported that at his death he "left volumes of verse, amounting, it is said, to nearly an hundred, prepared for the press."[3] Most of these manuscript works have disappeared, probably burned by his disciple Frederick Tatham who came to think that Blake had been inspired by the Devil. Only four works of any bulk survive in manuscript: *An Island in the Moon*, a prose

2 / *The Antijacobin Review*, XXXI (1808), 234, lamenting his dedicatory poem "To the Queen" in the 1808 edition of Blair's *Grave* bearing his designs. The three works quoted in Blake's lifetime are *Poetical Sketches* (1783), *Songs of Innocence and of Experience* (1789, 1794), and *Descriptive Catalogue* (1809) as well as "To the Queen," above.

3 / Allan Cunningham, *Lives of the Most Eminent British Painters, Sculptors, and Architects* (1830), II, p. 188.

burlesque on the intellectual fashions of 1783; *Vala* or *The Four Zoas*, a heroic poem of some four thousand lines, of 1795–1807;[4] The "Pickering (or Ballads) ms," a fair copy of poems made about 1803;[5] and his *Notebook* crammed from 1793 to 1818 with poems, epigrams, and memoranda. The problems with these works in manuscript are much like those for other writers. The seventy leaves of *The Four Zoas* were left loose and unsorted, and they exhibit frequent palimpsests and contradictory directions by Blake about rearranging his poem. The *Notebook* and *The Four Zoas* have paper of several kinds in the same manuscript, some leaves showing fragments of printed letters, and both show additions of different but yet indeterminate date on the same page. There are complicated, intriguing, and occasionally very beautiful drawings which sometimes clearly illuminate the words on the page and sometimes seem to be quite irrelevant. Except for the drawings, Blake's manuscripts present the same kinds of problems as those of other authors.

Blake's writings were originally printed in only five books set from movable types, but all these present special problems to the editor. One, *The French Revolution*, survives only in a unique proof copy. Two others – his first work, called *Poetical Sketches* and issued in 1783, and the *Descriptive Catalogue* of his Exhibition in 1809 – were apparently never "published" in the ordinary sense, and every copy known to have been disposed of by Blake has manuscript alterations. Even the two works published in the ordinary way present special difficulties, though fortunately the Blake works they contain are fairly ephemeral. A good deal is known about the first – B. H. Malkin's *Memoirs of his Child*, 1806; one thousand copies were printed, but it sold only about forty copies annually, and ten years later half the printing was pulped. The second – Blair's *Grave*, published

4 / Bentley, ed., *Vala or The Four Zoas* (1963).

5 / Bentley, "The Date of Blake's Pickering Manuscript," *Studies in Bibliography*, XIX, (1966).

with illustrations and a dedicatory poem by Blake in 1808, suffers from the opposite disability; it was so popular that there were two editions within the year, and no one has established clearly which is the earliest.

Finally, there are Blake's works in his unique method of illuminated printing. For these, Blake etched the words and designs in relief on copperplates, printed the plates in ink which he made himself, watercoloured the designs with the help of his wife, stitched the leaves together, and sold the work. He bought his paper and copper, but every other step of the process was completely in his hands, from conception to advertisement and sale. He preserved the copperplates and printed from some of them for almost forty years – indeed, a few were printed on paper watermarked 1831 and 1832, four and five years after his death. The colour of the printing ink is green, red, blue, yellow, brown, or black in different copies; Blake deliberately made the watercolouring of each copy unique; at least two variant and authoritative page-orders are found in almost every work in illuminated printing; and Blake made important changes in design and in text during the printing process – by wiping the plate or masking it – or afterwards by hand – with ink or watercolour. As a consequence, no two copies of works in illuminated printing which Blake sold are identical, and many seem to illustrate all the changes of Proteus.

Therefore, the first step in establishing a text is to examine every traceable copy of each work by Blake in ms or in print (excluding the exceptional works published commercially, such as Blair's *Grave*). This is not such a formidable task as it might at first appear, for Blake's works are not very common. By comparison, Shakespeare folios are a glut on the market, and even complete Gutenberg Bibles are easier to find than some of Blake's printed works, six of which survive in unique copies. All together, for twenty-eight titles which Blake printed, only about two hundred and sixty copies survive; of these, fifty-six are defective, missing one or more integral leaves, and at least sixteen were printed posthumously.[6] The most commonplace is *Songs of Innocence and of Experience*, of which I have seen twenty-seven copies printed by Blake himself. To these should perhaps be added twenty-three copies of the separately issued *Songs of Innocence*. The other twenty-six titles average only six complete copies apiece.

This relative scarcity of Blake's works reduces from impossible to manageable the problems of seeing all surviving copies. Enquiries at several hundred libraries have established that Blake's originals are scattered in over eighty collections, from Auckland to Los Angeles to Stoke-on-Trent. Seventeen copies of which some record survives still elude me, but some of these have not been mentioned in print for over one hundred and fifty years. For the rest, I have personally examined every known copy of each printed work, except for four books and some fragments, chiefly in Australia and New Zealand, which I have had to record through microfilm and correspondence.

I have enormously enjoyed the process of locating and seeing the copies of Blake's works. During the search I have been welcomed in Park Avenue apartments and thatched cottages, in shops and museums from San Francisco to Paris. More often than not I brought away as much in friendship as in knowledge from these visits. The pleasure of handling beautiful and long-sought (sometimes long-lost) works is sufficient incentive in itself. In Mr Rosenwald's Alverthorpe Gallery or in Mr Mellon's Oak Spring, one can handle in luxury and leisure copy after copy of works worth more than their author earned in his entire lifetime. Elsewhere, the public librarian or private owner may solicitously turn each page for you – which is likely to complicate somewhat the problem of recording watermarks and offsets.

The pleasures of the chase are fascinating in themselves. One

6 / In addition, there are some 376 plates of fragments, mostly either early proofs or posthumous copies, which considerably complicate matters.

North American family has misplaced three works worth an African dictator's ransom and has not been able to trace them for twenty-five years. A mid-western museum had for twenty-five years a copy of *Songs of Innocence* without realizing that it was an original until I came upon it in a kind of lumber-room. It had been catalogued as a facsimile. A manuscript letter, untraced for thirty-five years, turned up in 1967 on deposit in the British Museum. A unique proof of Blake's *Europe*, which went to earth in 1938, surfaced recently in the collection of a friend. A defective copy of Blake's *Poetical Sketches*, which disappeared in 1941, was unexpectedly sent to me for an opinion a few years ago, and is now in the University of Toronto Library, the only contemporary copy of Blake's works in Canada. A new though minor manuscript turned up between the composition and the printing of this paper. Each original found differs from all others previously known and provides a little more evidence as to how Blake intended his works to reach the public.

What kinds of conclusions flow from such an examination? The simplest ones concern the works in conventional typography: the *Poetical Sketches* and the *Descriptive Catalogue*. Of the latter, seventeen copies are recorded, and of these two are untraced. The work contained only two important errors which Blake wanted to correct. On page 64, the words "idea of want" should have been "want of idea." More important, on the title-page there was no indication of where the exhibition described could be seen, so at the bottom he wrote: "At N[*umber*] 28 Corner of Broad Street Golden Square." Blake made these two changes in exactly the same way in nine of the sixteen copies examined.[7] Probably he made the changes in all the copies of the *Descriptive Catalogue* which he left at the exhibition in his brother's shop, to be sold to viewers for 2s. 6d. These copies sold

7 / Copy O (untraced) has its variants recorded and titlepage reproduced in G. Keynes, *Blake Studies* (1949). On p. 45 of copy K, the "s" of "opinions" has been deleted, but the absence of other corrections, and the fact that copy K was acquired by Linnell in 1831, suggest that the change was made later than the others, and perhaps not by Blake.

were, therefore, in a sense issued as corrected. The uncorrected copies he presumably kept by him and gave away to such friends as he thought might still be interested even after the exhibition had closed. There is some evidence to support this conclusion. Three of the seven uncorrected copies are known to have belonged to men who did not meet Blake until eight years or more after the end of the exhibition in 1810, and one of them has a presentation inscription of 1824. The corrected state of the *Descriptive Catalogue* is therefore the earliest one as issued, and the uncorrected state left Blake's hands later.

Blake was nothing like so systematic with his *Poetical Sketches*, printed in 1783. Twenty-two copies are recorded, one of them untraced and four of them defective. Of the twenty-one copies examined, eleven have manuscript alterations neatly lettered in by Blake. Of the ten virgin copies, one is exactly in the state in which it must have come from the press – unstabbed, uncovered, the pages untrimmed, the sheets uncut, laid loose in quires, not even folded. Blake evidently kept a good many copies in this state, for his disciple Samuel Palmer had at least "*3* copies . . . *in sheets*."[8] While they were kept thus, the last two or three quires were apparently damaged, for these last sheets were replaced in facsimile in four copies of *Poetical Sketches* before 1783 (copies K, L, P, U). None of the five copies evidently preserved in sheets long after Blake's death has any manuscript changes. Probably Blake made alterations when he was disposing of a stabbed copy. It seems likely that the ten copies which survive without manuscript additions are therefore in a sense "posthumous" copies, which did not leave his possession until after his death. The uncorrected state of the *Poetical Sketches*, like that for the *Descriptive Catalogue*, is that which left Blake's hands last.

Blake clearly gave away the *Poetical Sketches* all his life, for three copies have inscriptions dating them in 1783 and 1784, while one belonged to John Linnell whom Blake did not meet

8 / According to the note in copy G made by John Linnell, Jr.

until thirty-five years later. He made a total of sixteen changes,[9] but he made them very unsystematically. Only one alteration appears in every corrected copy, and ten of the alterations appear in only one or two copies. Only two copies have identical sets of corrections, and both were given away in 1783 by Blake's intimate friend John Flaxman. It is surely plain that Blake did not have a master plan for correcting the book, and that he merely glanced over it each time he disposed of a copy and altered what caught his eye.

The changes range from improvement of punctuation and correction of gender and agreement to the redrafting of half a stanza. The only change he made consistently was the alteration of an erotic image (evidently a misprint) to a pastoral one: "rustling beds of dawn" to "rustling birds of dawn." Even changes which seem vital to the sense appear to have been made almost at random. For example, the last word in the fourth line of the "Mad Song" is clearly wrong:

> The wild winds weep,
> And the night is a-cold;
> Come hither, Sleep,
> And my griefs unfold.

The sense demands that the griefs should be concealed, not displayed, but in only two copies did Blake alter "unfold" to "infold".

There is nothing like a master-copy of the *Poetical Sketches* with all the changes incorporated. The most heavily annotated copy yet omits seven changes made in other copies. It is possible to establish some order of priority among the copies, with the help of inscriptions and information about early ownership, but the pattern of correction still appears erratic. Blake made about the same number of changes in late copies as in early ones; they were just different changes. The best one can do in the circumstances is to establish the approximate date at which copies were

9 / Keynes, *Blake Studies,* notes ten changes in six named copies.

corrected and note precisely which copies contain which corrections.

The most perplexing problems are raised by the fact that Blake was his own printer and illuminator. Since the works were ordinarily printed on single leaves, the techniques and terminology of analytical bibliography are rarely very applicable. The closest analogy is in stereotype printing, whether from fused or cast typefaces as in, say, prayerbooks, or from copperplates, such as Rembrandt's etchings or much early music-printing. Unfortunately the methodology of analysis in these areas is not very highly developed, and generally the Blake editor must devise his own techniques.

The problem is that any portion of any plate could be changed by Blake at any time throughout his life. A page printed in conventional typography may have perhaps 1,500 units of type which can be altered either individually or in relationship to each other, but on engraved plates the number is infinite. I believe that the most accurate method of discovering changes would have been to make an exact-size photographic colour-transparency which could be laid over the original so that the differences could be compared precisely. Even this, however, would have posed a number of problems. For one thing, the bulk of equipment to be carried to each original would have been formidable and the cost prohibitive – well over $2,000. For another, the colouring of each copy is different, and the colours in the transparency might have seriously obscured the original. And finally, some, perhaps many, owners would not be pleased to have their precious and delicate originals handled as much as this process would necessarily entail. I therefore took what I still believe to be the only practicable alternative. I had black-and-white xerox copies made of specimen originals of each work in illuminated printing, and if possible of posthumous black-and-white copies showing the works in their latest states. These xeroxes I carried with me always, laying them beside the originals and examining each section of the prints comparatively with a magnifying glass.[10] I am satisfied that the method has permitted me more confidence in my conclusions than has heretofore been possible, and that only some mechanical method of superimposition will improve upon it. Perhaps more accurate colour-microfilms than are now obtainable, compared on an improved Hinman collator, would be the answer.

Not long ago it was discovered that the extant copies of one of Blake's best-known prints, the frontispiece to *Europe* known as "The Ancient of Days," were made from two quite distinct copperplates. It occurred to me that other such unsuspected duplicates might be detected by millimetric differences in plate size, and I made thousands of such measurements. This laborious idiot-work demonstrated nothing more than that, over a couple of centuries, paper can shrink or stretch a couple of millimetres.[11] I found no more duplicated plates.

I have also tried to be meticulous in recording the colours of inks and watercolours used, and this has been more rewarding. I do not pretend that this was carried out with maximum scientific precision, however. For one thing, the ISCC-NBS colour charts were not available when I began the work, and their predecessors were impracticably bulky and expensive. For another, Blake's colours are elusive; the printing ink on a single page will vary in shade depending upon how thickly it was laid on, how much was wiped off, how much pressure was used in printing, how many impressions were taken before it was re-inked,[12] and how much it has faded in the ensuing decades. It is entirely possible that quite a number of shades of gray for example,

10 / A Hinman collator would not be practicable at present, both because the colours would interfere with each other and because it would be virtually impossible to get two originals side by side in the machine, and too dangerous to use even one at a time.

11 / I am certain about this shrinking and stretching, for I have compared original prints from Blake's *Grave* designs with the surviving copperplates in the Rosenwald Collection.

12 / I am persuaded that Blake ordinarily blotted the ink, or took a trial proof, before printing the final copy, so that the ink on the copper was rarely entirely fresh.

represent the same original shade of black in Blake's inkpot. Of course, the watercolours added to the designs afterwards vary far more. One lightly coloured plate might well have thirty shades on it, discontinuously distributed, and another copy of the same plate with the same shades could have them distributed entirely differently. After having used the ISCC-NBS color charts, I am persuaded that such precision would multiply the labour many-fold with only minimal unique advantages. Such terms as "dark bluish-Green," which in fact are used in the colour charts, are sufficient for present purposes; no previous attempt had been made to record in detail, even in such general language, the colouring of individual copies.

Some useful conclusions emerge from this colour record, particularly with the *Songs of Innocence and of Experience*, where the sample is comparatively large. In the early copies,[13] the designs are normally coloured lightly while the text is not touched with watercolour. In the other, later, copies a watercolour wash has been added to the text as well as to the designs, often splendidly enhancing the artistic effect of the page as a whole and making parts of the text almost illegible. This colouring feature may thus be a very useful indicator of date, the colouring of the text beginning perhaps about 1802, thirteen years after *Songs of Innocence* first appeared.

Even more precise as an indicator is the colouring of certain individual plates. In "The Little Black Boy," from *Songs of Innocence*, the little black boy says:

> My mother bore me in the southern wild,
> And I am black, but O! my soul is white.
> White as an angel is the English child:
> But I am black as if bereav'd of light.

In early copies, to about 1798, both children are coloured pink, presumably representing their state "When I from black and

13 / *Innocence*, copies A–M, P–R, U; *Innocence and Experience*, copies A–D, F–H, J, K, X.

he from white cloud free,/And round the tent of God like lambs we joy." In later copies the child at Christ's knee is pink, while the child at a distance is black.

Similarly, in "The Little Girl Lost" the lost girl is "seven summers old" in the text, but the design shows her as a clothed adolescent in the arms of a young man. In early copies, the poem is bound with *Songs of Innocence* and the young man is naked; in later copies the poem is bound with *Songs of Experience* and the young man is decorously clothed in blue. The colour change took place later than that in "The Little Black Boy," after a few copies of *Songs of Innocence and of Experience* had been printed, but thereafter it is fairly consistent. Such evidence as this from colours can sometimes be very helpful in dating copies, in demonstrating that individual plates in a given copy were printed at different times, or in showing that leaves from separate copies have been accidentally mingled.

One of the most vexing problems facing a Blake editor is the arrangement of the leaves in a given work. The *Songs of Innocence*, for example, seems to have the plates arranged by Blake in thirty-seven different ways. About 1818 he wrote out "The Order in which the Songs of Innocence & of Experience ought to be paged," but only one copy is bound to conform to it. No more than six contemporary copies were arranged alike. Further, two poems, "Laughing Song" and "A Dream," were first bound with *Songs of Innocence* in 1789, were later put with the first few copies of *Songs of Experience* made about 1794, and were returned to *Songs of Innocence* in all other copies. It would be comforting to be able to see a little order in this apparent anarchy.

It is true that the order of the plates in the *Songs* is extraordinarily various, but the arrangement of the leaves is far more constant. The first eighteen copies of *Songs of Innocence* (copies A-M) and of *Songs of Innocence and of Experience* (copies B-F) have the plates printed on both sides of the leaf, and, while the order in which the leaves are bound varies, the plates printed back-to-back on the same leaf are quite regular. On about ninety per cent of the leaves, the same plates are printed on recto and verso. Thus "A Dream" and the first plate of "The Little Girl Lost" are regularly found on the same leaf, and "The Tyger" and "London" are always found back-to-back. A few of these leaves were bound almost indifferently with one plate or the other as recto;[14] for example, half the time "London" appears on the recto of its leaf and half the time "The Tyger" is recto. On the other hand, most of the leaves are almost always bound with the same plate as recto;[15] "A Dream" always precedes "The Little Girl Lost" on the leaf. Further, there are four poems in *Songs of Innocence* – "The Little Black Boy," "Spring," "The Little Girl Lost," and "The Little Girl Found" – which were etched on two plates printed on separate leaves. Obviously these two leaves had to be bound contiguously in order not to separate the halves of the poems.[16] Thus the position of most of the poems is defined in relation to their immediate neighbours, if not more precisely in the over-all order.

These plates printed back-to-back on the same leaf explain why "A Dream" and the "Laughing Song" were transferred from *Songs of Innocence* to *Songs of Experience* and then back again. The move was fairly clearly an accident accompanying a deliberate transfer. As soon as he began to print *Songs of Experience* in 1794, Blake included in it the two poems ("The Little Girl Lost" and "The Little Girl Found") which had been printed on three plates in *Songs of Innocence* during the previous five years. Thereafter, these two poems never appear in *Songs of Innocence* again. However, on the recto of the first leaf

14 / The leaves with plates (8, 11), (18, 12), (38, 41), (39, 44), (42, 46).

15 / The leaves with plates (6–7), (15, 9), (10, 54), (13–14), (16–17), (24, 19), (20–21), (27, 22), (23, 53), (26, 34), (35–36), (30–31), (32, a), (40, 49), (48, 51).

16 / In *Innocence* copy P, however, the second plates of "The Little Black Boy" and "A Cradle Song" are missing, and the catchwords are deleted as if to show that the change was deliberate.

of "The Little Girl Lost" Blake normally printed "A Dream," which was never intended as a poem of *Experience*, but which had to follow "The Little Girl[s]" into *Experience* willy nilly. Recognizing the problem eventually, Blake tried to put another poem on the recto of "The Little Girl Lost," but he chose the "Laughing Song" from *Songs of Innocence* rather than an appropriate one from *Experience*. Indeed, in all copies of *Songs of Experience* with plates printed back-to-back on the same leaf, Blake printed a song from *Innocence* on the recto of the "Little Girl Lost" leaf, while neither "A Dream" nor the "Laughing Song" appears in any copy of *Experience* in which the leaves are printed on one side only. It is therefore reasonably clear that while "The Little Girl Lost" and "The Little Girl Found" were deliberately bound with *Songs of Experience*, the "Laughing Song" and "A Dream" are only found there by an accident of printing.

The greatest technical problem which faces an editor of Blake's writings is how to reproduce works in illuminated printing. Each plate of the original has some design, and many plates are largely or entirely design. Obviously, it would be most desirable to choose a clear black-and-white copy text for each work and reproduce it in facsimile. This raises a number of formidable difficulties, however. For some works every copy is heavily coloured, and it is not possible to see Blake's etched lines clearly. The plate-size varies from 1½ by 2 inches to 7 by 9 inches, a variety which would make any publisher blanch, and has made mine do so repeatedly. It would be quite difficult to attach notes or page and line numbers to a facsimile page. Perhaps most awkward, some of Blake's text is quite difficult to read, even in the original. Not only did he often colour over the text, but in his epics *Milton* and *Jerusalem* there are sometimes sixty lines to a page, and the letters are very small and crowded. The best solution, I believe, is to give the text in ordinary typography, but to insert reproductions of the designs in the places Blake gave them in his text. This method would give maximum legibility and convenience of annotation with the closest feasible approximation to the union of text and design which Blake intended. I hope an edition of Blake's writings will appear in this form some day.

I warned at the beginning that I was more generously supplied with problems than with solutions. Many of the most characteristic difficulties presented by Blake's text seem to me to be *sui generis*. Perhaps the most perplexing difficulty for an editor trying to establish a stable text is that Blake's poems and their designs do not hold still. They alter from copy to copy in the most disconcerting way, each variation beautiful and complete unto itself. Even the works printed from movable types were changed in each copy that left Blake's hands, and the illuminated works vary in colouring, page-order, wording, and designs. The best an editor can hope to do is to record the changes in Blake's text, if possible in chronological order, if possible with some explanation of the reasons for the individual changes, and, occasionally, with an indication of a steady development. Like those who struggled with old Proteus, Blake's editors can scarcely expect unqualified success, but they can anticipate exhilaration from the variety of the struggle.

[This paper, originally scheduled for delivery at the Editorial Problems Conference, was cancelled when I was unexpectedly called to Algeria as a Fulbright Professor at the last moment (August), and then re-instated when the paper which was to replace it was suddenly and unexpectedly withdrawn. "William Blake's Protean Text" was therefore written among date palms at the foot of the Atlas Mountains and kindly read at the conference by my good friend, Professor D. I. B. Smith. It thus violated the protocol of the conference, which requires the authors to stand to their texts under questioning from the learned audience. I hope, however, that this enforced distance of author from auditor will not affect the arguments of the revised paper.]

The Ledgers of William Strahan

O M BRACK, JR.

The State of my Family and Business is briefly this. My eldest Son William is now, you know settled by himself, and will, I dare say, do very well; tho' the Printing Trade is by no means a very profitable one. It requires great Industry, Oeconomy, Perseverance, and Address, to make any great Figure in it. . . . My youngest Andrew is the only one now with me, and from whom I receive any Assistance in Business. But his Time is almost totally taken up in the Printing-house, in looking after 7, 8, or 9 Presses, which are constantly employed there: For besides the Chronicle and Monthly Review, I have always a pretty large Share of Book-work, in many Articles of which I am myself a Proprietor. – I have also one half of the Law Printing-house which is kept, separately, at some Distance from my own House; and as my partner in that, Mr. Woodfall, died about two Years ago, the whole Care of it lies upon me. – As doth the Management of the King's Printing-house, My Partner Mr. Eyre not being bred to the Business, and being in the Country. – It is true, we have distinct Overseers for both these Branches, to take Care of the Conduct of the Business within Doors. But still the general Management, and the Accounts, of all these Branches, falls to my Share, in which I cannot easily receive much Assistance from any body. Add to all this, the Multiplicity of Concerns I have in the Property of Books (above 200 in Number) which require, every one of them, some Attention, and a separate and distinct Account, and a Variety of Avocations which cannot be particularly enumerated, the Correspondencies I am unavoidably drawn into, and engaged in, and the Share and Attention I am often obliged to take and bestow in the Concerns of others; – I say when you consider all these Particulars, you may naturally conclude that my Time is pretty fully engrossed.[1]

In this oft-quoted letter, written by William Strahan at the height of his career in 1771 to David Hall, one finds a graphic view of the activities at what Samuel Johnson called the "greatest printing house in London."[2] Although a close analysis of Strahan's business records and various other documents about printers and printing of the period indicate that his printing business was operated in much the same way as the other printing houses of the period (except perhaps, on a larger scale), Strahan was no ordinary printer. In a letter of 22 February 1772 Hume wrote:

As we are drawing near a Conclusion [reading proofs on the new edition of the *History*], I cannot forbear giving you many and hearty thanks, both for your submitting to so troublesome a Method of printing and for the many useful Corrections you have sent me. I suppose, since the days of Aldus, Reuchlin, and Stevens, there have been no Printers who could have been useful to their Authors in this particular. I shall scarcely ever think of correcting any more. . . .[3]

Edward Gibbon paid Strahan no less a compliment in his *Memoirs of my Life and Writings.*

1 / William Strahan to David Hall, June 15, 1771, David Hall Collection, Historical Society of Pennsylvania. Published in *The Pennsylvania Magazine of History and Biography*, XII (1888), 116–17.

2 / *The Letters of Samuel Johnson*, ed. R. W. Chapman (Oxford, 1952), II, p. 23.

3 / *Letters of David Hume*, ed. J. Y. T. Greig (Oxford, 1932), II, p. 259.

After the perilous adventure had been declined by my friend Mr. Elmsly, I agreed, upon easy terms, with Mr. Thomas Cadell, a respectable bookseller, and Mr. William Strahan, an eminent printer; and they undertook the care and risk of the publication, which derived more credit from the name of the shop than from that of the author. The last revisal of the proofs was submitted to my vigilance; and many blemishes of style, which had been invisible in the manuscript, were discovered and corrected in the printed sheet. So moderate were our hopes, that the original impression had been stinted to five hundred copies, till the number was doubled by the prophetic taste of Mr. Strahan. . . . The first impression was exhausted in a few days; a second and third edition were scarcely adequate to the demand; and the booksellers' property was twice invaded by the pirates of Dublin.[4]

Or as Benjamin Franklin reminded Strahan, with obvious satisfaction, in one of his last letters to him:

I remember your observing once to me, as we sat together in the House of Commons, that no two journeymen printers within your knowledge had met with such success in the world as ourselves. You were then at the head of your profession, and soon afterwards became a Member of Parliament; I was agent for a few provinces, and now act for them all. But we have risen by different modes. I, as a republican printer, always liked a form well *planed down*, being averse to those *overbearing* letters that hold their heads so *high* as to hinder their neighbors from appearing. You, as a monarchist, chose to work upon *crown* paper, and found it profitable; while I worked upon *pro patria* (often indeed called *fools-cap*) with no less advantage. Both our *heaps hold out* very well, and we seem likely to make a pretty good day's work of it.[5]

These passages represent only a few of the many contem-

4 / *The Memoirs of the Life of Edward Gibbon*, ed. G. B. Hill (London, 1900), pp. 194–95.

5 / *Life and Writings of Benjamin Franklin*, ed. Albert H. Smyth (New York, 1906), IX, p. 262.

porary testimonies that might be cited to authenticate the extraordinary success of Strahan, a success he achieved not only because of his astute business sense, but also because of his ability to earn the esteem of literary figures as well as of members of the trade. Strahan's career as publisher and bookseller has already been amply set forth in the various studies of Robert Harlan, whose work has shown us the singular importance of Strahan's printing ledgers.[6] But these ledgers not only tell us about Strahan; they also provide the most complete extant record of printing practices in the eighteenth century, dealing as they do with the works of Johnson, Fielding, Thomson, Gibbon, Hume, Robertson, Smith, and Smollet, to name only a few of the more obvious authors. Yet these ledgers, which exist in ten volumes of manuscripts in the British Museum, are presently available only in microfilm at a few libraries in the world.

Clearly enough, then, the ledgers are virtually inaccessible. Until they are readily available in printed form, they cannot be studied by eighteenth-century bibliographers; and until they are annotated as fully as possible, they cannot be profitably used by eighteenth-century researchers of any kind. I am proposing, then, to undertake a compilation of the information in the ledgers, with William B. Todd of the University of Texas and Patricia Hernlund of Wayne State University, and the purpose of my present remarks is to set forth the rationale of our procedure.

The general printing ledgers from which the compilation will be made can be summarized as follows: ledger A, the earliest extant, contains entries from November 1738 to June 1776, with the majority of the entries falling between 1739 and 1768. If Patricia Hernlund's analysis of Strahan's bookkeeping methods is correct, this is the only surviving ledger which appears in final form: that is, in double entries without crossing out or checking off to indicate the entries having been trans-

6 / See particularly his unpublished dissertation (Michigan, 1960), "William Strahan: Eighteenth Century London Printer and Publisher."

ferred to another ledger.[7] Until about 1750 the entries are rather complete. For example, a complete entry for a book would give an accurate date, the title of the work (the volume and the edition of the work when relevant), the number of sheets printed, the type employed, the format, the number of copies printed, the kind of paper used, the price per sheet, and the total cost of the printing.

1743
April 2 For printing the first Volume of Fielding's
[A39d] Miscellanies 26 ½ sheets Pica 8vo.
No. 1000 coarse and 250 fine @ £1-2-6 £29-16-0

After this period, the entries become abbreviated and usually give only the approximate date of the entry, the title of the work, the number of sheets printed, the number of copies printed, the price per sheet and the total cost of the printing. The following entry is typical of the later period:

1761
Febry 12 Tancred and Sigismunda, 5 ½ sheets
[A120h] 750 @ £1-0-0 £5-10-0

As will be seen shortly, the abbreviated entries will create a number of interpretative problems.

Only each opening of the ledger is numbered in the upper right-hand corner, as was Strahan's habit; the debits are listed under the publisher's name on the left-hand page and the credits are listed on the right-hand page. At the beginning of the ledger is an alphabetical table of contents of the publishers contained in the volume. (ledgers B, D, F, and G have almost similar tables but contain, in addition, most of the books entered in each volume.)

7 / See her unpublished dissertation (Chicago, 1965), "William Strahan, Printer: His Career and Business Procedures." Also her article, "William Strahan's Ledgers: Standard Charges for Printing, 1738–1785," *Studies in Bibliography*, XX (1967), 89–111. Another possibility is that the other ledgers have a different style of bookkeeping with cross-outs merely indicating payment.

This does not seem to be the earliest record Strahan kept, however, because an entry on opening 6c, dated 16 August 1739, indicates that he *reprinted* George Whitefield's "Second Journal."[8] This work is not mentioned previously in ledger A. Strahan himself told Johnson on one occasion that " 'the first book he had ever published was the *Duke of Berwick's Life*, by which he had lost: and he hated the name' "[9] It seems probable that this work can be identified as the *Life of James Fitz-James, Duke of Berwick* published by Andrew Millar in 1738. Also there is some evidence that Strahan may have been printing in partnership with T. Hart as early as 1737.[10]

Ledger B contains entries primarily from 1752 to 1770 with a few entries as late as 1776. This ledger, with a few exceptions, is chronologically filled out with block entries crossed out to indicate, most likely, their having been transferred to another ledger. (Many of the entries, for example, were transferred to ledger D.) A typical entry from ledger B would read:

1754	Partners in Rod. Random	
Aug.	Printing do. 26 sheets No. 1000	
[B9c]	@ £1-8-0	£36-8-0
	copy of do. to print by	£4-0
	paid March 22, 1755[11]	

This ledger also contains a list of apprentices bound between 1739 and 1771; birth, marriage, and death dates for Strahan's family; birth and death dates for some of his friends, including "Mr. S. Johnson."

Ledger C contains entries from 1765 to 1768. This is a small

8 / There is a possibility, of course, that this is a reprint of another printer's work. I have not been able at this point to establish with any degree of certainty that the first edition was printed by Strahan.

9 / *Boswell's Life of Johnson*, ed. G. B. Hill and L. F. Powell (Oxford, 1934), III, p. 286.

10 / R. A. Austen-Leigh, "William Strahan and his Ledgers," *Library*, ser. 4, III (1923), 265.

11 / When payment is noted, the entry is cancelled.

ledger, apparently a gathering from a more extensive ledger now lost, containing only 13 leaves with the entries in block style crossed out. This ledger is in very rough state, is not in chronological order, and contains no table of contents.

Ledger D contains entries from January 1768 to March 1785 and forms a continuous sequence with ledger A and ledgers E and F. The ledger is mostly in account style, that is, the entries are double-entry, and are therefore close to final form. The remainder of the entries are in block style. Many of the entries are crossed out.

Ledger E is in part duplicated and extended by ledger F. Ledger E contains entries from January 1777 to November 1783 while ledger F contains entries from January 1777 to March 1790. As has been pointed out, these ledgers form a continuous sequence with ledger A and ledger D. Again, the entries are in account and block style with many of the entries crossed out or checked off.

Ledger G contains entries from October 1765 to September 1791 with the majority of the entries falling before 1786. Most of the accounts are not checked off or crossed out but rather signed by Strahan and the customer directly on the page.

In addition to the general printing ledgers which will make up the body of the compilation, the following ledgers will most likely be included as appendices: ledger H, a cash book recording cash received and cash disbursed from January 1777 to 3 February 1801, and ledger J, a list of copies taken from 1739 to 1778; ledger K, a volume which contains debts owed to Strahan and debts owed by Strahan from 1771 to 1784, and gives us the state of his business at four different periods: 1 January 1771, 1 January 1773, 1 January 1776, and 1 January 1780; and finally, ledger L, a summary of Strahan's business and personal expenses from 4 August 1739 to December 1783.

The body of the compilation will consist of four elaborate indices to the information contained in the general printing ledgers, A through G. The primary index will incorporate the whole publishing history for the works printed by Strahan and will enable the reader to find all the information about a work, now scattered through several ledgers, under one heading. A sample entry would be as follows:

J17 Johnson, Samuel. *Dictionary.*
B10f. *Do.* [1st. ed.] April 55. Printing 580 sheets, No. 2000 @ £1-18-0 per sheet, £1102-0-0. Two Red Titles, £1-18-0. Paid for Alterations and Additions, £132-10-0. A98a. *Do.* [2nd. ed] June 55. Printing 5000 Proposals in Folio, £3-8-0. 24000 in Quarto @ £0-5-0, £6-0-0. 250 Folio Titles to stick up, £0-2-6. 50 Advertisements for Country Papers, with Paper, £0-5-0. Composing half a sheet Brevier for *London Magazine,* £1-4-0. Printing 38 sheets, No. 2298 @ £2-0-6, £76-19-0; 174 sheets, No. 1274 @ £1-10-6, £265-7-0; 367 sheets, No. 768 @ £1-6-0, £477-2-0. For two Red Titles, £1-13-0. For printing 50 Reams of Blue Covers @ £0-5-5, £12-10-0. . . . B16u. [1st. ed. 8°] Dec. 55. Printing 70 sheets, No. 5000 @ £4-5-0, £297-10-0.[12]

After all of the works have been arranged alphabetically by author, if the author can be ascertained, and if not, alphabetically by title, a work-index number will be assigned to be used for cross-referencing. "J17" is the hypothetical work-index number for Johnson's *Dictionary.* "B10f" gives the location of

12 / This sample contains only a small amount of the material available in the ledgers on Johnson's *Dictionary.* The complete entry would give in chronological order the printing history of all the editions printed by Strahan.

the entry in the ledgers. "B" is the ledger letter reference (see table I), "10" is the number of the opening, and "f" means it is the sixth entry in the opening. Next, the edition of the work in question is identified, if at all possible, and the date of the entry is given. This is followed by the entry as it appears in the ledger with regularization when necessary to make the information clear.

TABLE I

B.M. Add. Mss	Microfilm Letter Reference (Original Negative at Bodleian)	General Description	Dates
48800	A	printing	1738–[1768]*–1776
48802A	B	printing	1752–[1770]–1776
48802B	C	printing	1765–1768
48803	D	printing	1768–1785
48810	E	printing	1777–1783
48809	F	printing	1777–1790
48806	G	printing	1765–[1786]–1791
48828	H	cash received	1777–1801
48205	J	copies taken	1739–1778
48808	K	account of estate	1771–1784
48801	L	general expense	1739–1783

*The majority of the entries in the ledgers fall before the date enclosed in brackets.

Needless to say, all of Strahan's time was not spent printing books. He, like many printers of his day, filled in the time between major printing work with "job" printing. Bills, receipts, catalogues, advertisements, labels, etc. were printed in abundance. All of this work will be entered in the primary index under subject headings, for example, advertisements for various products; causes and events will simply be listed under "Advertisements" by surname and then chronologically, rather than being listed separately. Road bills will be listed under that heading alphabetically by place, and so on. Also included in this category for the purpose of indexing will be the various "Trials" and "Cases" [non-legal] to be listed under that heading even if the work can be identified. Work by a known author, however, would be listed under that author, for example "Fielding" for *A True State of the Case of Bosavern Penlez.*

The second index will be a concordance which will allow the reader to reconstruct the entries on any given page. A hypothetical representation of openings 98 and 99 of ledger A would appear as follows:

A		A	
98a	J17	99a	R25
		b	M7
		c	T22
		d	F3
		e	L22
		.	
		.	
		.	
		bb	Z1

Opening 98 of ledger A has only one entry – that for the second edition of Johnson's *Dictionary* – while opening 99 has twenty-eight entries, all identified by work-index numbers.

The third index will be a reconstruction which will summarize the previous data and give all the data concerning the business transactions for printing not given above. In other words, this index will be primarily a financial summary.

A99a–bb. D. Wilson and T. Durham
Nov. 53-5 Sept. 57. £332-12-1½
Credit notes: 8 Dec. 55. By
3 *Smellie's Midwifery*, 2 vol. bound,
£1-7-9. By *Rowe's Letters* and *Mason's Odes*, £0-3-0. 31 Mar. 56.
By *Forbe's Works*, £0-4-6. . . .
6 Aug. 56. By ½ Paper for 3rd.
ed. *Smellie's Midwifery*, Vol. I,
58 Reams @ £0-18-0, £17-18-0. . . .
11 Jan. 57. By Cash on acct.,

> £80-0-0. 12 Feb. 57. By Do.,
> £20-0-0. 4 June 57. By a Bill
> on Messrs Hamilton and Balfour,
> £10-0-0. . . .

In ledger A, opening 99, there are twenty-eight entries between November 1753 and 5 September 1757 to the account of D. Wilson and T. Durham, totalling £332 12s. 1½d. The remainder of the entry is the credit information (selected, in this case) as it appears in the ledger, with some regularization to make the information clear.

Finally, all of the information contained in both the general printing ledgers A through G and the ledgers H through L included in the appendices, with the exception of the authors included in the primary index, will be brought together in a general index.[13]

The most important and most difficult task in this compilation will be the exact identification of the books entered in the ledgers. To indicate some of the problems involved in identifying these books I will take an obvious example. At opening 65m in ledger A, under the name of Andrew Millar, appears the following entry for January 1749:

Foundling 81 sheets No. 2000 with many Alterations,
@ £1-15-0 £141-15-0

We do not know the author's name, of course, since Strahan did not bother to mention it when he made the entry in his ledger. Where do we go from here? A hurried look at the *British Museum Catalogue of Printed Books* under "Foundling" and "Foundlings" gives us no help. Of the nine entries under "Foundling" and the two under "Foundlings" only one title seems helpful but in fact it would only lead us astray. It is *"A*

13 / This section concerned with the presentation of the information in the ledgers has been considerably revised since the paper was presented at the conference. I am particularly indebted to my collaborators, William B. Todd and Patricia Hernlund, and to Donald Eddy, John M. Robson and Francess Halpenny for many suggested revisions.

Criticism of the Foundling . . . in a Letter to the Author. London. 1748." This "Foundling" turns out to be Edward Moore's comedy produced at the Theatre Royal, Drury Lane, February 13, 1747–48. A look at the *Cambridge Bibliography of English Literature* and Block's *English Novel* still fails to give us a lead. Since Strahan usually gives very brief titles to the works entered in his ledgers and often merely descriptive titles such as "Six letters on baptism" for Henry Mayo's *The True Scripture Doctrine Regarding Baptism*, or simply "Mr. Farmer's Sermon" (one is likely to find that there are a number of Mr. Farmers writing sermons on any number of topics), we are certainly justified in being suspicious that this is not an accurate title for the work in question. Obviously then, the next step is to attempt to establish, as closely as possible, the exact title of the work and hopefully discover the identity of the author. As announcements of publication are most likely to give this information, a search must be made through the magazines and newspapers of the period. We begin by searching the magazines such as the *Gentleman's Magazine*, the *London Magazine*, and the *Monthly Review* simply because they are more readily available and easier to use than the newspapers. The newspapers, obviously, will have to be searched for the more difficult items. At any rate in this instance we do not have to search far, since the *Gentleman's Magazine* for February 1749, has the following entry, item number 47 under "Register of Books": "The history of Tom Jones, a foundling. By H. Fielding, Esq; in 6 vols. 18s. Millar." Now we go back to the *British Museum Catalogue of Printed Books*, look under "Henry Fielding," and verify the title. In this case the title in the *Gentleman's Magazine* is correct but this is not always so. For example, in the May 1749 issue of the *Gentleman's Magazine*, Smollett's tragedy, *The Regicide* appears as "*The Regicide*; *or, James the first of Scotland. A tragedy*. pr. 5s. Osborne." In the June 1749 issue, the tragedy is announced as "*The Regicide; a tragedy*. By the author of *Roderic Random*. 1s. 6d. Osborne." In all copies of the tragedy which I have seen, the subscription issue (May) and the trade issue (June) have the same title and only the imprint differs. Although the title of the tragedy is correct (except for capitalization and punctuation) in the advertisement for the subscription issue, its title page, in fact, also contains the phrase "By the author of Roderick Random" but does not contain Osborne's name in the imprint as does the trade issue which, of course, in the advertisement has the title of the tragedy given incorrectly. In other words, no matter which of the advertisements you choose you are likely to be led astray. Hence, the need for verifying the accuracy of the title.

Perhaps all of this seems simple enough, but what about *Nurse Truelove's Christmas Box*, a publication consisting of one half-sheet printed in an astounding edition of 14,000 copies in February 1749 or 1750? John Newbery published it and, of course, William Strahan printed it, but who wrote it and what is it about? Is it akin to "*The Christmas Box; consisting of moral stories, adapted to the capacities of little children, and calculated to give them early impressions of piety and virtue* . . . in 2 vols., adorned with cuts" advertised in the *Gentleman's Magazine* for December 1749 or is it, as Freudian interpretation of the title might suggest, more adult fare? My researches to date have turned up one copy of *Nurse Truelove's Christmas Box; or, The Golden Plaything for Little Children, by which they may learn the letters as soon as they can speak, and know how to behave so as to make everybody love them*, but it is an undated edition printed for "T. Carman and F. Newbery, jun." As Francis, the son of John Newbery, did not come into the business until after his father's death in 1767, this edition is obviously a later reprint. Perhaps all 14,000 copies of the earlier edition have disappeared without a trace.

Then there is an entry made to the account of John and James Rivington during March 1752 with the seemingly unlikely title of "Dog's Plea." I say "seemingly unlikely" because I have been able to find some references to "Dog's Plea." These

Mr. John Newbery Dr.

1745		£	s	d
April	For printing a Spelling Dictionary 4½ Sheets Brevier 32s. No. 2000 @ £3:7s p Sheet	15	1	6
Sepr. 14	For printing Advertisements, a Broad Side No. 1000		17	6
Octr.	For printing the Art of Poetry 8½ Sheets 32s. No. 2000 @ £2:10s p Sheet	[illegible]	5	6
Decr.	For printing 2 Sheets of Corderius No. 2000 @ £2:18 p Sheet	5	16	—
	For 4 Reams of Paper furnished for Do.	1	12	—
March	For printing ~~300~~ 250 Proposals for Songs	1	[illegible]	6
	For printing 500 Bills for Indian Snuff		5	
	For printing 500 Covers for Songs, with Catalogue for No. 1		10	6
	For printing 3 Sheets of Corderius No. 2000 @ £2:5 p Sheet	6	15	—
	For printing Covers for Songs for 8 Numbers, 500 each	1	—	
	For 4 Reams of Pot Paper, with Carriage 2d.	1	9	6
1746	For your Share of the Loss on the Courier	2	3	6
Febry	For 300 Bills of the Use of the Powder		7	6
1747 March	For printing Scheme for Manning 20 Ships of War, ½ Sheet, No. 500	2	16	—
1748 Jany	For your Share of the 3d Edition of the Little Book for Children	7	6	—
	For 1500 Titles to Circle of Sciences with Paper		15	—
	For Printing Directions for the Powders No. 6000 (2 4to & 2 8vo)	2	5	—
	For Labells for Do. No. 20000	1	5	—
March	For Dissertation on Fevers 3½ Sheets No. 2000 @ £1:10:0 p Sheet	5	5	—
	For printing Directions for Jackson's Tincture No. 2000, with [illegible] Covers	1	[illegible]	—
	For 1000 More Do.		5	—
April	For 2000 More Do.		10	—
August	For 2000 more, with alterations	1	5	—
Decr.	For James's Dictionary in Quires	4	10	—
	For a further Call on British Magazine	5	5	—
	For Your Share of Loss upon Do. at settling the Acct.	9	2	1
	For Mosley's Poems in Quires 3 vols		12	—
	Nurse Truelove's Christmas box ½ Sheet No. 14000 ([illegible])	5	15	6
Febry	Nurse Truelove's New years Gift one Sheet No. 6000	5	14	—
	The Cavalier Detected 2 Sheets No. 500	1	8	—
June	To James's Dictionary Do.	5	5	—
19	For printing a Collection of Epigrams 3 Sheets No. 2000 @ £2	6		
	Proposals for Mr. Smart's Poems No. 250 with Paper		7	6
	Receipts for Do. No. 400 with Paper		5	
Jany	4000 Quarto Bills for the Lilliputian Magazine	1		
	Progress of Envy, a Poem, 3½ Sheets No. 500 @ 12s. ([illegible])	2	2	—
	Lilliputian Magazine No. 1. 2 Sheets No. 4000 @ £2:15 p Sheet	5	10	—
	Cover for Do. ½ a Sheet No. 4000	1	7	6
	8000 Proposals for Do.	1	10	—
	No. 2 Do. 2 Sheets No. 4000	5	10	—
	Cover for Do. ½ Sheet No. 4000	1	7	6
	~~Preface to the Uncertainty of the Signs of Death ½ Sheet No. 1000~~			
	~~For a Ream of Paper for Do.~~			
	4000 Letters for Lilliputian Magazine in 4to	1		—
1752 Febry	Description of May by Gawen Douglas 5½ Sheets No. 600 @ 14s.	3	17	—
June	Smart's Poems 31 Sheets No. 1000 @ 18s.	27	18	—
	Extra for Subscribers Names of Do. Recomposed and Altered	1	9	—
		166	17	7

William Strahan's printing ledgers: opening 55 of ledger A; British Museum Add. Ms. 48800 are references to *The Dog's Plea: or reasons most humbly submitted by the barking fraternity of Great Britain, to the men their masters. Shewing why dogs ought to be exempted from taxes*, by Brindle but published for Griffiths and mentioned in both the *Gentleman's Magazine* and the *Monthly Review* for March 1753. There is also the *Insincere Professor* printed in an edition of 500 copies for Richard Hett in July, 1748 and the *Letter to the Fool* printed in an edition of 500 copies for John and James Rivington in November 1752. To date I have been unable to locate references or copies for either of these and there are dozens more just as enigmatic.

Additional difficulties arise with interpretation of the information for each entry as the entries become more abbreviated, for example, in the entry for "Tancred and Sigismunda" on 12 February 1761. The exact date on which this work was printed is conjectural. This entry appears third in a series of four works printed for Andrew Millar on this date. It seems extremely unlikely that four works were printed for him on the same day. It seems rather more likely that the "12 Febry" applies only to the date of printing the first work in the series with the other works being printed later the same month, since below this group of entries appears another group of four entries with the first of that series simply labelled "March." These entries are not terribly difficult to interpret, however, because it does seem that we have them pinned down to the month and year. But John Newbery's account in ledger A, opening 55 (see figure 1) for the years 1749 through 1751 is a different matter. This section of the account could be variously interpreted as follows: (a) the February and June entries are for 1749 and the January entries are for 1750, which means that nothing was printed for Newbery in 1751; (b) the February and June entries are for 1750 and the January entries are for 1751, which means that nothing was printed for Newbery in 1749; (c) the February and June entries are for 1749 and the January entries are for 1751, which means that nothing was printed for Newbery in 1750. (a) is true; (b) is true; (c) is true; all of the above are true; none of the above are true. I am certain that most of these entries will be puzzled out but it is clear that the dates will be of very little assistance. At least in one instance it seems that Strahan did not make an entry in his ledger until the printing, including its corrections and alterations, had been finished. Strahan's ledger records the first printing of Johnson's *Journey to the Western Islands of Scotland* in January 1775 although Johnson's correspondence mentions the printing as early as the previous July.[14] Strahan's failure to be scrupulous in dating his entries may be puzzling to a twentieth-century scholar who is used to paying most of his own bills within thirty days, but a quick glance at almost any of the credit pages will indicate that Strahan was seldom paid within six months after completion of his work for a client and probably thought the exact date unnecessary.

Similar ambiguities may arise, though fewer in number, as a result of Strahan's failure to give the edition, the format, or the kind of paper used.

Of course, one would like to have all the books in the ledgers carefully identified as to author, title, publisher, date of publication, and edition. This is the ideal, but realistically there is a strong likelihood that there is much job work for which the ledgers serve as the only record. There will be another category of printing entered in the ledgers and announced as published by the various magazines and newspapers of the period but for which no copy can be located. How large these categories will be I am hesitant at this time to say. Keith I. D. Maslen, in his study of the ledgers of William Bowyer[15] acknowledged that he was unable to locate 279 out of the 1,806 books listed, after a search through the thirteen principal libraries in and around

14 / Chapman, *Letters*, I, p. 410.

15 / A copy of Keith I. D. Maslen's unpublished dissertation is in the Bodleian Library.

London. This is some fifteen per cent of the whole and includes a number of popular works such as Tipper's *Ladies Diary* for 1760, printed in 15,000 copies. This does not look encouraging.

The primary index, then, if it is to be of any real value, must take all of these categories into account. The books for which copies can be located, with the authors and titles verified, will be entered under the name of the author, if that can be established, and under the title if it can not. In addition to the correct author and title, the publisher, date of publication, and, when it seems necessary and is possible to ascertain, the edition will be given in the index. These entries will be printed in roman type. The next category of books in the index will be entered under author or title as in the category above, but the information will be taken from the announcements of publication in the magazines and newspapers of the period. These entries will be printed within single quotation marks. The final category of books, hopefully small – those for which no information can be found – will be entered as they appear in the ledgers, usually under the title, since the author is seldom given. These entries will be enclosed in double quotation marks. This index, then, will serve as a short-title list for all work printed by William Strahan.

The usefulness of the printing ledgers of William Strahan has been demonstrated long ago. As early as 1917, for example, J. Paul de Castro used the ledgers to prove that the edition of Fielding's *Journal of a Voyage to Lisbon*, which appeared in ten sheets, was in fact the first edition although it did not appear until after the second edition in twelve sheets.[16] William B. Todd, in addition to other evidence, used information in the ledgers to show that Johnson's *Taxation no Tyranny* not only existed in four "editions" all printed in March 1775, but that the second edition, thought to be suppressed, did in fact run to

16 / J. Paul de Castro, "The Printing of Fielding's Works," *Library*, ser. 4, I (1921), 268–69.

twice the number of any other edition and had only been hiding under the title of the first.[17] James Sledd and Gwin Kolb drew heavily on the ledgers to trace the progress of Johnson's *Dictionary* after 1749.[18]

The necessity for eighteenth-century bibliographers to examine not only contemporary notices in magazines and newspapers of the books described, but also the relevant entries in the Strahan and Bowyer ledgers, was aptly shown in Professor Todd's brief analysis of the bibliography of the Wesleys. He found that the bibliography recorded "no separate printing of *Swear Not at All* . . . no Strahan editions of 15 other works which he lists as printed, no editions whatever of 14 other books exclusively entrusted to Strahan, none of 3 others which, it would appear, the Wesleys edited, and none at all by Mrs. Wesley, though she apparently wrote at least one pamphlet. Moreover, as the ledger indicates, the bibliography has incorrectly dated John Wesley's *Hymns for Times of Trouble*, and has arranged in the wrong order the editions of his *Hymns on God's Everlasting Love*."[19]

As an index to the taste of the Age of Johnson, the ledgers have not been tapped. Richard Altick, in his chapters on the mass reading public in the eighteenth century in *The English Common Reader*, does not mention Strahan,[20] but as Professor Todd has shown, in his *New Adventures Among Old Books*, the Great Cham, as literary arbiter of the age, has misled us somewhat about the literary fashions of the day. "Notwithstanding Samuel Johnson's pronouncements, most of his contemporaries seem to have had quite different tastes, preferring in the drama,

17 / William B. Todd, "Concealed Editions of Samuel Johnson," *Book Collector* II (1953), 49–65.

18 / James H. Sledd and Gwin J. Kolb, *Dr. Johnson's Dictionary; Essays in the Biography of a Book* (Chicago, 1955).

19 / William B. Todd, *New Adventures Among Old Books* (Lawrence, Kansas, 1959), p. 17.

20 / Richard Altick, *The English Common Reader* (Chicago, 1957), pp. 30–77.

Otway's *Orphan* (9,000 copies in three editions), in the novel, Fielding's *Tom Jones* (10,000 copies in four editions), in poetry, Thomson's *Seasons* (13,240 copies in seven editions)."[21] There were the numerous Methodist publications – literally dozens of titles, in thousands of copies. John Wesley's little pamphlet, *Swear Not at All*, was printed in seven editions of 21,000 copies and a pamphlet, *A Word in Season*, was printed in three editions of 9,000 copies in two months. The most extensive run in the ledgers is the proposal for the *New Universal Dictionary* printed in three editions in 1775 and totalling 134,000 copies. This is a startling figure in light of Edmund Burke's reported estimate that the English reading public included in 1790 some 80,000 persons.[22]

As was indicated earlier, the printing ledgers of William Strahan are the most complete record extant of eighteenth-century printing. From what we know about eighteenth-century printing, from Richardson, Bowyer, various printing manuals, and other documents of the period, we know that Strahan's shop seems to be typical of his age. Hence, the ledger will be a standard reference to the printing procedures of the eighteenth century for the bibliographer and historian of printing.

Finally, in more optimistic moments, it is hoped that this edition of the printing ledgers of William Strahan will serve as a basis for what now seems to be only the dream of eighteenth-century scholars – a Short-Title Catalogue of Books Printed in the Eighteenth Century.

21 / Todd, *Adventures*, pp. 16–17.
22 / Preface to the first volume of the *Penny Magazine* (1832).

Literature in the Law Courts, 1770-1800

WILLIAM J. HOWARD

LIKE THE Glorious Revolution of 1688, the Act for the Encouragement of Learning (1710, 8 Anne, c.19 (21)) was a feasible solution to a very complex question. It did not resolve any theoretical questions about the radical nature of copyright nor did it accomplish anything more than the provision of an extremely ambiguous precedent. But the act was a beginning. Because it was an act of parliament, it officially released the booksellers and authors from the constricting regulations of the Company of Stationers; publishing became a lucrative profession; and copyrights developed into valuable private assets.

In 1731, after the expiration of the twenty-one year period protecting works published before the passing of the act, older copyrights – monopolies, as some saw them – were the cause of frequent litigation between rival booksellers, or between booksellers and printers aspiring to the financial rewards of a bookseller. I have located approximately thirty-three cases, between 1731 and the end of the century, that contest the question in one form or another. A good deal of further evidence indicates that booksellers and authors prepared cases which for one reason or another never reached the court. The latter half of the eighteenth century was the experimental period during which the interested parties: authors, booksellers, lawyers, and judges, analyzed the situation in order to resolve two complex questions: what was the nature of copyright? and what were the equitable solutions to the problems it raised? Various aspects of the "great question" are interesting because they were responsible for the modification of minor genres within the tradition of English literature. The entire controversy is important because it is an influence that must be acknowledged in an analysis of the transition between eighteenth- and early nineteenth-century writing.

I feel that one can fairly simplify the historical complexity of the many proposed answers into four theoretical solutions. The first theory was that the protection of a publication was a natural right and was only made statutory by 8 Anne, c.19. The Statute was an added protection for authors over a period of time and then it ceased so that society might have free access to their works. The second theory was that the protection of copyright was a legal monopoly granted by parliament for a set period to protect and encourage writing by means of a financial reward; nevertheless, any idea, once published, belonged to all men. Thirdly, copyright was either a natural right or it was a monopoly based on labour, judgment, and expense. And fourthly, copyright was either a natural right or it was a monopoly on certain sentiments clothed in a specific set of words. These solutions appear in every possible set of combinations and each answer had an effect upon publishing practices and ultimately upon authors.

The tension between the first two solutions was resolved quite simply. In 1763 the bookseller Taylor sold the rights for Thomson's *Seasons* to Andrew Millar; but because, under the terms of 8 Anne, c.19, the protection of *The Seasons* had expired, Taylor himself reprinted the work the same year. In 1766 Millar sued Taylor in the court of the Kings Bench and in 1769 the judges rendered their decision, although divided, in favour of Millar and the principle that copyright was a natural and perpetual human right. A second case involved the same principles but with the opposite conclusion. In 1767 Alexander Donaldson of Edinburgh reprinted Thomas Stackhouse's *History of the Bible*, its protection having ended in 1760. In 1770 Hinton sued Donaldson in the Scottish court of Sessions and on 20 July 1773 a decision was rendered in favour of Donaldson; one judge was favourable to the idea of perpetual copyright and eleven were against it. The issue was finally resolved in 1774 after Donaldson appealed an injunction against his right to publish an edition of Thomson's *Seasons*, the House of Lords deciding in favour of the natural right to protection of copy but concluding that the right should be terminated for the benefit of society after the protection provided by the act had expired.

Although the difference between the natural-right solution and the constituted-monopoly solution was thus resolved in 1774, the influence which the constituted-monopoly solution exercised on publishing practices is inestimable. The influence became especially strong because of the uncertainty created by the next pair of answers derived from an attempt to establish the radical nature of copyright. The conflict in this case derived from the important practical implications of each position. One solution, the oldest and best accepted in the annals of both law and literature, established copyright on the principles of labour, judgment, and expense. The second solution defined copyright as a natural relationship which existed between the author and his work because the sentiment, the ideas, and the language were uniquely his. At first implicit but becoming more explicit, the uniqueness and the originality of sentiments expressed, and the uniqueness and originality of the specific set of words used were emphasized.

I have just stated that the older and better established answer founded the right to copy on labour, judgment, and expense. For a very fully developed history of this position, no better document exists than the transcript of the trial of *Millar* v.

Taylor ((1769), 4 Burr. 2303). Briefly, the argument is this: all printing was introduced into the kingdom at the expense of the king; therefore, the crown has the legal right to control publishing and any profits accruing from publishing. Furthermore, certain areas of study – for example, law and religion – were directly the concern of the king who therefore had the right to control publications in those areas. If he wished to share this right with individuals, giving them a monopoly over certain works as a form of reward, he could do so. Because of the nature of English case law, personal copyright in the eighteenth century, was solidly aligned with and supported by the history and judgments rendered in the seventeenth century based on the arguments for the crown's property rights, derived from expense, judgment, and labour. In the early eighteenth century the arguments were used successfully in favour of personal copyrights against the censorship of the crown and the monopolies granted by the crown, and then against the Stationers' company in favour of individuals.

As I have explained elsewhere, it was from this theoretical basis that another series of judgments developed, supporting the whole eighteenth-century practice of abridgments, translations, and compilations.[1] Whether these appeared as new and independent works or in the periodical press, juridically they could claim the right to protection because of the expense, labour, and judgment involved. Well-respected authors saw

1 / The legal decision was to my knowledge first rendered in favour of a translation when the judge agreed with the argument that a translation "... in some respects may be called a different book ... that the translator dresses it up and clothes the sense in his own style and expressions, and at least puts it into a different form from the original and *forma dat esse rei*." (*Burnett* v. *Chetwood*, 1720, Chan. xv. 441 (Chan.)) But throughout the eighteenth century it was also applied to abridgments, the usual wording running something like this: "... the abridgment must be a fair one, and not a colourable shortening of the work." (*Dodsley* v. *Kinnersley*, 1761.) See Wm. J. Howard, "Dr. Johnson on Abridgment – A Re-examination," *P.B.S.A.*, LX, 215–219.

these judgments and this practice not only as the status quo but as a desirable practice in need of protection.[2]

Because abuses multiplied, because of the very questionable practices in which some authors, booksellers, and the publishers of periodicals were engaging, other authors withdrew their support from this principle. Authors were republishing their own works in new settings; other booksellers were editing and abridging their works. If a work were a popular success it was immediately abridged, edited, imitated, criticized, reproduced in every form until the public tired of it.[3] The constant litigations, the accusations and cross-accusations over questions of abridgments, compilations, and imitations caused a general distaste for the practice, both in the law courts and among authors. Virtually every court case begins with the tired observation that "This is a question that has often appeared in this court for judgment." In an extended note, which I should like to quote at length, from *A Letter to W. Mason* by a bookseller the chaotic state of the practice is summed up very well. The work is an answer to Mason's accusation that the bookseller had pirated Gray's works. In it, the author begins by making some telling points, which can be supported from external evidence, against Mason's own publishing practices. Then as a final *reduxio* against the idea of challenging compilations or abridgments he writes:

2 / Cf. eg., *The Works of Samuel Johnson*, ed. Arthur Murphy (London, 1823), xi, pp. 34–35; *The Collected Letters of Oliver Goldsmith*, ed. Katherine C. Balderston (Cambridge, 1928), pp. 51, 73; Oliver Goldsmith, *The Preface to the History of England* in *The Works of Oliver Goldsmith*, ed. J. W. Gibbs (London, 1884), v, pp. 168–69. These are but a few of the many examples.

3 / Goldsmith, *Works*, v. pp. 166–67, 257; i, pp. 245, 246, iii, pp. 282–87, 356–57, 453, 509. *New Essays by Oliver Goldsmith*, ed. R. S. Crane (Chicago, 1927), pp. xxi, 98–103, 135. *Diary and Letters of Madame D'Arblay* (1778–1840), ed. Charlotte Barrett (London, 1905), iii, pp. 127–29. *The Letters of Thomas Gray*, ed. Duncan C. Tovey (London, 1912), ii, p. 77. *The Letters of Tobias Smollett*, ed. Edward S. Noyes (Cambridge, Mass., 1924), p. 67–68.

Mr. T. Cadwell, bookseller in the Strand, will not, surely, be accused of encouraging Literary Piracy; yet has this gentleman published a book, entitled, "An Historical Miscellany," which consists entirely of large Extracts from authors, whose works, at this moment, are considered to be property, viz. Hume, Robertson, Ferguson, Lyttelton, Scrafton, Voltaire, Dalrymple, Burke, Hampton, Leland, Smith, etc., etc. Similar to this work are the *Moral Miscellany*, and *Poetical Miscellany*, printed for the same bookseller; Dr. Enfield's "Speaker," printed for Mr. Johnson; and an hundred collections of the same kind. If Mr. Mason is right in his prosecution, this practice, hitherto considered as legal, must be abolished; and *Collections* of all kinds, whether for the use of schools or not, be totally prohibited.

This event, if it takes place, affords a noble field for litigation, as, besides the articles above mentioned, Lord Kaim's *Elements of Criticism*, Dodsley's *Collection of Poems* and *Fugitive Pieces*, Pearche's *Collection of Poems*, Dilly's *Repository*, every *Collection of Songs* (and these last are without number), will fall under this prohibition. And the profits of every edition for many years back, must be accounted for. A fruitful prospect for Gentlemen of the Law![4]

This note by no means overstates the distasteful state into which publishing practices had descended; the reason for the decline was the faulty basis upon which the judicature had established copyright.

The situation just described reached its most extreme degree between 1750 and 1780 and had a definite effect on authors; it helped modify certain types of writing which until the late eighteenth century were considered quite admirable forms of literary composition. If, for example, we examine a document like Hurd's "Discourse on Poetical Imitation" (1751), we see all the older values of the eighteenth century reflecting a veneration for the neoclassical tradition. His emphasis is still upon the

4 / (London, 1777), pp. 63–64.

judgment (*Works*, II, p. 231); invention is less important (p. 232); one assimilates and reworks older works to make the imitation surpass its original. This combined activity leads to an admirable original, he continues (p. 233). Then he adds the expected remark: "For when a writer, who, as we have seen, is driven by so many powerful motives to the imitation of preceding models, revolts against them all, and determines, at any rate, to be *original*, nothing can be expected but an awkward straining in every thing. *Improper method*, *forced conceits*, and *affected expression*, are the certain issue of such obstinacy."[5] The conclusion to his essay is well known but bears quotation in the light of the present discussion: "... Though many causes concur to produce a thorough degeneracy of taste in any country; yet the *principal*, ever, is, THIS ANXIOUS DREAD OF IMITATION IN POLITE AND CULTIVATED WRITERS. And, if such be the case, among the other uses of this Essay, it may perhaps serve for a seasonable admonition to the poets of our time, to relinquish their vain hopes of *originality*, and turn themselves to a stricter imitation of the best models."[6] The purpose, then, for the discourse was an exhortation to traditional methods and authors. Yet by 1757 the whole question seems to have shifted; I feel it is very possible to attribute this change to the contemporary practices of authors and booksellers, especially those engaged in abridgments and compilation. The transition is foreshadowed in the diction and the tone of such a statement as, "Coincidences of a certain kind, and in a certain degree, cannot fail to *convict* a writer of imitation."[7] Or again, "We frequently find some latent circumstance . . . that convicts him of imitation."[8] Finally, "Milton and Pope, if they have made but few poets, have made many imitators; so many, that we are ready to complain there is hardly an original poet left."[9]

5 / In *The Works of Richard Hurd* (London, 1811), II, p. 234.
6 / *Ibid.*, pp. 240–41.
7 / [Richard Hurd] *A Letter to Mr. Mason; on the Marks of Imitation* (Cambridge, 1757), p. 3.
8 / *Ibid.*, p. 54.
9 / *Ibid.*, p. 60.

If we compare these statements with many others written during the same period, I think we will recognize the immediate source for the reversal of Hurd's position. Goldsmith, for example, wrote:

It is usual for the booksellers here when a book has given universal pleasure upon one subject to bring out several more upon the same plan; . . . the first performance serves rather to awaken then satisfy attention; and when that is once moved, the merit of the first diffuses a light sufficient to illuminate the succeeding efforts; and no other subject can be relished, till that is exhausted.[10]

The quantity of derived material caused Hurd to reverse his position, or so another publication claimed. In *Reflections on Originality in Authors* (London, 1766), the author argued that when many men observe the same thing and write about it, one can expect the different works to be in some ways similar; one need not impute imitation as the cause. He then continues, "this rule seems universally to hold good; but in all cases where Imitation is expressly intended, or the Plagianism [*sic*] is so notorious as to admit no doubt of its reality."[11]

After the author laments that Hurd had condemned all modern literature as being without genius and derivative, he continues with a plea to recognize the originality of what is being written. He too tries to distinguish between what is good imitation and what is borrowed *verbatim*, and brands the latter as "plagiarism." This brief exchange was the death-knell of the practice of imitation though it continued to rest uneasily on the shoulders of the English author. The reason for this demise, I feel, was the malpractices of the later eighteenth-century publishing world, and the legal thinking which made those practices possible.

Writers at the end of the century began distinguishing between the practices of compilation, abridgment, and translation, and more unique efforts based on originality of ideas and

10 / *Works*, III, pp. 356–57. See also III, pp. 192, 193, 283, 287, 473, 504.
11 / Pp. 3–4.

the manner of their expression; the reason for this is not hard to discover. Works discussing copyright began making a strong distinction between the right based on labour and judgment, and the right based on a specific set of ideas in a specific set of words. Prior to the period we are examining, the most common argument developed in this manner: "We may derive a Property from the Ideas of others, not only by improving and adding to them, but merely by employing more Labour on them."[12] If we follow the debate through the seventies and eighties, this distinction grows stronger; the principle based on labour moves from being favoured to being tolerated, from being tolerated to being rejected.[13]

This same movement is reflected in the works of authors, although less clearly. For example, the advertisement for a two-volume abridgment of Gibbon's *Decline and Fall*, published in 1789 by G. Kearsley, expresses the author's uncertain position quite well. "Although but little merit can be ascribed to an abridgment, yet much presumption may be imputed to the present attempt to contract a work that has been received with universal admiration. The author, who now subjects these pages to the perusal of a candid public, is sensible of the delicacy of his situation."[14] And well might he be, for the legal thinking was changing rapidly in its treatment of the right-based-on-labour

12 / [William Flexheny], *A Letter from an Author to a Member of Parliament* . . . (London, 1762). See also Alexander Donaldson *Some Thoughts on the State of Literary Property* . . . (London, 1764); *Considerations on the Nature and Origin of Literary Property* (Edinburgh, 1767).

13 / *Speeches and Arguments of the Judges* . . . (London, 1769), p. 4; *Millar* v. *Taylor*, 4 Burr. 2310; *Observations Occasioned by the Contest about Literary Property* (Cambridge, 1770), pp. 5–10; *Observations on the Case of the Booksellers of London and Westminster* (London, n.d. [1774]; [James Burrow] *The Question Concerning Literary Property Determined . . . 1769* (London, 1773), p. 10.

14 / Goldsmith was even more to the point when he wrote: "Above all things, I would advise you to consult the original historians in every relation. Abridgers, compilers, commentators, and critics, are in general only fit to fill the mind with unnecessary anecdotes, or lead its researches astray." *Works*, v, 257.

principle. Ever so slowly one can notice a new element introduced into the litigation. Ignored at first, gradually, between 1761 and 1801, it gained advocates; it emphasized the simple Latin word *verbatim*.

In the case of *Dodsley* v. *Kinnersley* (1761), there was no question of Johnson's lawyer using a *verbatim* argument against the abridgment of *Rasselas*; his argument rested on the fact that the best parts, the moral reflections, had been edited from the abridgment and only the plot remained. This was his only course of action because in 1761 the one successful argument against the abridgment rested on the fact that the abridgment devalued rather than enhanced Johnson's novel. By 1785, in the case of *Bell* v. *Walker*, the lawyer for the plaintiff used the *verbatim* argument unsuccessfully. "Passages were read from each, to show that the facts, and even the terms in which they were related in this, were taken frequently *verbatim* from the original work." The argument was unsuccessful because of previous precedents; the judge considered the work a *bona fide* abridgment.[15]

By 1801 the argument was being used very seriously and had won more support in judicial quarters. During the case of *Butterworth* v. *Robinson* (5 Ves. cc. p. 709) the council for the plaintiff argued that the *Abridgment of Cases* was a mere *verbatim* copy, the cases reported being merely alphabetized rather than arranged chronologically. The judge rendered a decision against the abridgment as an extremely illiberal publication; this is a definite development from the judgment that accepted a reprinting as original simply because it deleted moral reflections! In another case, begun in 1799, the principle was developed more completely. In an extended litigation over road books, the point on which the judges based their decision has become the question: does the work improve or add to existing scholarship?[16]

15 / 1 Bro. CC. 451.

16 / See Lord Mansfield's decision as recorded in *Cary* v. *Longman* (1 East, 358).

Because the trade practice had badly tarnished the value of the original theoretical principle based on labour and judgment, and because the courts were having a difficult time deciding which abridgment was a new work and which was a colourable piracy, both the legal profession and authors began to favour the second theoretical basis for copyright – a certain set of ideas clothed in a specific set of words. The great trials of the seventies, along with the writings they provoked, are responsible for this triumph.

Previously, the theoretical justification which tried to found a property right on a certain set of ideas clothed in a specific set of words, being too tenuous a concept, was weaker and more often and easily challenged. I have found no example of its being used as a legal defence in a court case. The first time the idea received a full treatment was in Warburton's *A Letter from an Author To a Member of Parliament* (London, 1742).[17] Thereafter it was repeated again and again.[18] It worked its way into the annals of legal theory through a very subtle but nevertheless traceable shift from the principle of expense, labour, and judgment to that of invention, labour, and judgment and was yoked to the expression "unique sentiments and language" in Blackstone's *Commentaries*. Blackstone wrote: "When a man by the exertion of his rational powers has produced an *original work*, he has clearly a right to dispose of that identical work as he pleases, and any attempt to take it from him, or *vary the disposition he has made of it*, is an invasion of his right to property. Now the identity of a literary composition consists *intirely in the sentiment and the language*."[19]

17 / P. 5 ff.

18 / See *A Vindication of the Exclusive Rights of Authors to their own Works* (London, 1762); *Speeches and Arguments of the Judges . . .*, p. 27; *Millar* v. *Taylor* (4 Burr. 2303). *Observations Occasioned by the Contest . . .*, p. 15 ff; *The Decision of the Court of Sessions . . .*, 7 Geo III, c.38; 17 Geo III, c.57.

19 / *Commentaries on the Laws of England* (Oxford, 1766), I, pp. 404–5.

Only after Blackstone officially sanctioned the terms invention, labour, and judgment, and yoked this phrase to the idea of specific sentiments in a specific set of words, did the younger theory begin to thrive. But between 1766 when the *Commentaries* were published, and the end of the century, this idea was to become the most frequently discussed and published theory in any single legal controversy about literature since the invention of printing. During the seventies and eighties this idea took firm hold on the minds of both the public and authors. The trials were surrounded by innumerable individual publications. Accounts of the arguments were carried as the lead articles in the *Gentleman's Magazine* for February, March, and April of 1774. Many authors followed the proceedings and quite a few have recorded their position on the question. James Burrow described the situation accurately when he wrote in the advertisement to one of his accounts:

> But, as it will require some Length of Time before a Folio-Volume of such a Work can be rendered fit for Public View, I have been applied to by several of my Friends who bear no small Character in the learned World, to select this case concerning Literary Property, and communicate it to the Public as a detached Piece by itself.
>
> The Subject of it is very interesting to Men of Letters, and important to the general Cause of Learning and Science.[20]

Nor can we discount the background against which this contest took place – the popular mentality to which the booksellers catered. Booksellers and the public wanted works which were new and different. A competitive press and the pressure of public taste prepared the way for a movement toward originality.[21]

But to return to the main development between 1770 and

20 / *The Question concerning Literary Property.*

21 / Goldsmith, *Works*, III, pp. 74, 192–93, 282–85, 356–57; Hurd *Discourse*, p. 234–35, 240–41, *Reflections on Originality* p. 6 ff.

1780: the supremacy of "the specific ideas in a specific set of words" was clearly accepted as the basis of the relationship between an author and his work. As one among many writers expressed it:

Every man has a mode of combining and expressing his ideas peculiar to himself. . . . A strong resemblance of style, of sentiment, of plan and disposition will be frequently found; but there is such an infinite variety in the modes of thinking and writing as well as in the extent and connection of ideas, as in the use and arrangements of words, that a literary work *really* original, like the human face, will always have some singularities, some lines, some features, to characterize it, and to fix and establish its identity.[22]

Moreover, between 1770 and 1780 writers came to the realization that if a natural right existed, then the whole question of abstracts, abridgments, and compilations had to be reconsidered.[23] A new emphasis was placed on the difference between original and derivative work; furthermore, "specific ideas clothed in specific words" was expanded to include, first uniqueness, then originality based on uniqueness. This progression was quickly recognized as the basis for art and the hallmark of artistic genius and was immediately developed. As one writer expressed it: "In the works of original writers such as Shakespeare, Milton, &c. this property is sufficiently ascertained; but for one original writer that appears in the republic of letters, there are five hundred copyists and compilers."[24]

Perhaps the best single expression of the idea which, although earlier and satirically presented, is still closely connected with the copyright question, was recorded in a passage from *The Vicar of Wakefield.*

22 / Francis Hargrave, *An Argument in Defence of Literary Property* (London, 1774).

23 / *An Address to the Artists and Manufacturers of Great Britain* (London, 1774), p. 45.

24 / *An Address to the Artists and Manufacturers*, p. 46.

I sate down, and finding that the best things remained to be said on the wrong side, I resolved to write a book that should be wholly new. I therefore dressed up three paradoxes with some ingenuity. They were false, indeed, but they were new. The jewels of truth have been so often imparted by others, that nothing was left for me to impart but some splendid things, that, at a distance, looked every bit as well.[25]

The result of the "great literary question," then, was twofold. Because abridging, compiling, and translating were the hack-work of booksellers and magazine houses, in the future serious authors would hesitate to engage in any type of imitative writing. Authors, especially the poets of the early nineteenth century, began to adopt the new emphasis placed on the now quite respectable ideal of originality because, "a literary work *really* original, like the human face, will always have some singularities, some lines, some features, to characterize it, and to fix and establish its identity." Originality became the identifying expression of the author, an aesthetic creed, and later an ethos.

25 / *Works,* I, p. 157.

No Dull Duty: The Yale Edition of the Works of Samuel Johnson

DONALD GREENE

"LET US NOW be told no more of the dull duty of an editor." Johnson was of course talking (in rebuttal of Pope) about the problems of an eighteenth-century editor confronted with the quartos and folios of Shakespeare's plays, pointing out that "an emendatory critic would ill discharge his duty without qualities very different from dullness." The problems of preparing a reasonably complete edition of Johnson's own writings are not too often of this nature;[1] nevertheless they are sufficiently varied

1 / Though very pretty "emendatory" questions do arise. For instance, in the Latin poem "Post-Genitis" ("To Posterity") which Johnson included in *Marmor Norfolciense*, the word *calceatos* occurs, in the sense of "trampled." The editors of the 1941 edition of Johnson's *Poems* emended this to *calcatos*, on the ground that in classical Latin *calceatos* can only mean "shod." I argued with the editor of the *Poems* in the Yale edition, Professor McAdam, that this emendation was unjustified: the poem is supposed to be not classical but "monkish" Latin, some support may be found in Du Cange for a mediaeval use of "calcio" in the sense of "trample," and, most importantly, the passage occurs not once but twice, at different places in *Marmor*, with *calceatos* both times. Hence the error, if it is one, is probably Johnson's rather than the printer's. McAdam agreed, and printed *calceatos*. Alas for ingenuity! A copy of *Marmor* later turned up with *calceatos* (both occurrences) corrected in the margin to *calcatos* in Johnson's hand, and in my edition of *Marmor* (in the volume of *Political*

and demanding. His works are vast in bulk and often unwieldy in form – an English dictionary in two volumes folio, an eight-volume variorum edition of Shakespeare, several years of reports of the debates of the British parliament – and incredibly diverse in content and purpose. Sometimes they were hastily written to meet a deadline (the printer's boy waiting outside the door as Johnson scribbled away), carelessly printed, and probably not corrected in proof: the editor must vigilantly scrutinize them for possible error. Yet when Johnson had the opportunity to make revisions for later editions, he often made them copiously: the editor must take them all into account. Only a tiny fraction of his output has survived in manuscript to assist us in determining what he wished to appear in print; and where it does, the manuscript, in Johnson's extremely difficult hand, sometimes raises more questions than it answers.

Just *what* Johnson wrote is very far from being established. For many years he earned his living by journalism, unsigned and difficult to identify in the periodicals of the time; he was addicted to making clandestine contributions – prefaces, dedications, introductory paragraphs, footnotes, revisions, once (probably) a whole chapter of a novel – to his friends' publications; he ghosted perhaps forty sermons for ecclesiastical friends, at least a dozen of which still remain to be identified; he collaborated with others in composing a long set of lectures on English law delivered to the students of Oxford University and an even

Writings) I shall so have to print it. (Yet one wonders what Johnson's ms read; perhaps a friend pointed out the error to him after publication.)

Another crux is in *A Journey to the Western Islands of Scotland*. In a description of stormy weather at Dunvegan, all early editions read, "The sea being broken by a multitude of islands, does not roar with so much noise, nor beat the storm with such foamy violence, as I have remarked on the coast of Sussex." R. W. Chapman was so much disturbed by the expression "beat the storm" that he emended it to "beat the shore." A later editor reluctantly retained "storm," explaining that, awkward as the expression is, the ocean *could* be regarded as contending with the storm on an open beach. But a simpler reading seems possible; readers may like to try their hands at deciphering it (hint: is "storm" an object or a subject?)

longer set of speeches placed in the mouths of the members of parliament of the time, and where Johnson's share in the collaboration begins and ends is not easy to decide. If, as someone has laid down, the first step in editing an author's works is to determine the "canon," an edition of Johnson might never be feasible, for the establishment of an agreed-on canon seems a very distant prospect indeed.

Nevertheless the need to make the bulk of the work of so great a writer easily available to the student and the "common reader" has been apparent from the time of Johnson's death in 1784. An attempt to supply this need was made in 1787, when a syndicate of the leading London booksellers issued *The Works of Samuel Johnson, LL.D.* in eleven substantial octavo volumes. The first of these contained Sir John Hawkins's unjustly abused *Life of Johnson*, and hence students have sometimes referred to the collection as "Hawkins's edition." This is a misnomer. Hawkins did contribute some notes to *The Lives of the Poets*, and Bennet Langton is supposed to have had something to do with bringing together Johnson's verse; but it is unlikely that the collection was ever really "edited" at all in the modern sense – the contents were probably desultorily assembled by some "house editor." To supply its obvious deficiencies, other enterprising publishers quickly brought out "supplementary volumes." In the same year, Stockdale added "Volumes XII and XIII," containing a mangled and incomplete set of the parliamentary debates,[2] and in 1788 the interesting "Volume XIV," with items as important as *Marmor Norfolciense*, *A Compleat Vindication of the Licensers of the Stage*, and *Miscellaneous Observations on Macbeth.* In 1789, George Gleig edited another volume, containing the Lobo-Le Grand *Voyage to*

2 / Students using this and later reprints of it (including that in the 1825 Oxford *Works* of Johnson) should be warned that what is probably the most important and most interesting single debate that Johnson reported, that in the house of commons on February 13, 1741, on a motion to remove Walpole from office, is not included.

Abyssinia and a handful of short pieces. These fifteen volumes remained the basis of all subsequent eighteenth- and nineteenth-century "editions" of Johnson – the six- or nine- or twelve-volume sets found on the shelves of most libraries (occasionally compressed into two volumes in fine print).[3] They are little more than reprints in various formats of the 1787–1789 *Works*; they are all hopelessly inadequate, and differences among them, in content and quality, are minimal. A few small changes did occur: in 1792 Hawkins's *Life* was superseded by Arthur Murphy's much less valuable *Essay on the Life and Genius of Samuel Johnson* (with the result that this and later printings which included it are sometimes erroneously referred to as "Murphy's edition"); in 1806, 1816, and 1823, Alexander Chalmers made some intelligent additions and deletions of shorter pieces; the 1825 Oxford edition usefully includes the twenty-five *Sermons Left for Publication by John Taylor*, earlier published separately. The legend that the 1825 Oxford edition is "the best," however, originates in an entry in Lowndes's *Bibliographer's Manual*, 1834, where a notice of this edition is printed, in larger type, at the head of the list of editions of Johnson's *Works*, and a highly flattering description of it appended. But Lowndes's reviser, Henry Bohn, gives the game away in the second edition of the *Manual*, where he adds the note, "Lowndes has placed this edition first in compliment to his publisher" – Pickering, who, by no coincidence, was the publisher of both Lowndes's *Manual* and the 1825 Oxford edition. Textually and (apart from the inclusion of the *Sermons*) canonically, the 1825 Oxford *Works* is no better than several other nineteenth-century versions of the 1787 collection; its

3 / The last of these seems to be one in 16 volumes with the imprint "Troy, N.Y.: Pafraets Book Co., 1903 (Literary Club Edition)" – merely another reprint of the 1823 or 1825 collection. The Lamont Library at Harvard has a set of this bound in 8 volumes with the imprint "Cambridge, Mass.: Harvard Cooperative Society; New York: Bigelow, Smith, and Co. (New Cambridge Edition)."

sparse but sometimes useful annotation seems to be mostly[4] copied from Chalmers's 1823 edition.

In this disgraceful situation the matter stood until the third quarter of the twentieth century. Of course, the assurances of Macaulay and others that Johnson's writings are negligible, and that it is only as a personality, preserved in Boswell, that he is of interest and value, helped to maintain the status quo. Throughout this century and a half of neglect, to be sure, isolated attempts were made to edit individual works by Johnson properly. Alexander Chalmers's edition of the periodical essays in *The British Essayists* (1803) manifests a greater sense of editorial responsibility than was usual at the time; George Birkbeck Hill's *Rasselas* (1887), one of many "school editions" of this work, is a good example of Hill's talent for garrulous but not unintelligent annotation; R. W. Chapman's *Journey to the Western Islands of Scotland* (1924) and *Rasselas* (1927) show his usual concern for textual questions. Two later volumes, however, mark the beginning of the application to Johnson's works of serious modern standards of editing. Allen T. Hazen's *Johnson's Prefaces and Dedications* (New Haven, 1937; his Yale doctoral dissertation) is a small masterpiece, a demonstration of how much light can be thrown on the dark places in a writer's literary career by meticulous bibliographical technique and a keen understanding of the way books come into being. In 1941, David Nichol Smith of Oxford, completing a project he had commenced in 1913, and E. L. McAdam, Jr., of New York University, whose editorial work on Johnson's poetry had formed the basis of his Yale doctoral dissertation, collaborated to produce an excellent edition of *The Poems of Samuel Johnson* (Oxford). Two other fine pieces of editing connected with Johnson – L. F. Powell's revision of Hill's six-volume edition of Boswell's *Life* and R. W. Chapman's three-volume edition of Johnson's *Letters*, both in progress throughout the 1930s and 1940s although not completed until the early 1950s – gave addi-

4 / Perhaps wholly; I have not fully collated it.

tional strength to the conviction which began to grow among the community of Johnsonian scholars at the end of the second world war that the time was long overdue for attempting the first real edition of Johnson's collected works.[5]

It was very much a "grass roots" movement. Although Johnsonians are grateful to the Yale University Press for having (eventually) agreed to publish the edition, they sometimes permit themselves a wry smile when they encounter the widespread assumption that the Yale Johnson and the Yale Boswell are parallel enterprises. The Yale edition of the private papers of James Boswell was "big business" from the start, with the university and the McGraw-Hill publishing company combining their resources to purchase the Boswell manuscripts for a still undisclosed but very large sum of money, and then to try to recoup their investment by high-powered sales and advertising methods which succeeded in making at least the first volume of the trade edition a world-wide best-seller.[6] The Yale Johnson is unlikely to appear in a trade edition, and has never had any substantial backing from universities, foundations, or commercial publishing houses. The initiative for the project came from within the closely knit community of dedicated Johnsonian scholars and collectors. Credit is due to many individuals in that community for contributing to get the project under way; but perhaps one name ought to be singled out for special mention in making the edition feasible: that of Professor James L. Clifford of Columbia. Clifford's chief interest has been in the biography

5 / Another important stimulus was given by the formation at Somerville, New Jersey, of the great Johnsonian collection of Donald and Mary Hyde, who in 1948 acquired the R. B. Adam collection of Johnsoniana and have greatly added to it. Their generosity in permitting scholars the use of it is well known.

6 / A Yale Johnson editor who is also a Yale Boswell editor points out that it should in fairness be mentioned that, whatever may be the case with McGraw-Hill, Yale, far from recovering its investment, has expended a large additional sum to maintain the Boswell "office," where the papers are arranged, catalogued, and prepared for editing, and that the individual editors receive only minute token payments for their work.

rather than the writings of Johnson, and he has taken only an advisory, not an active editorial, role in the work of the edition. But it was his devotion, both personally and through his editorship of the *Johnsonian News Letter*, to the cause of creating and maintaining close liaison and fellowship among Johnsonian scholars throughout the world that made it possible for so extensive an undertaking to be realized on a basis of voluntary, unpaid co-operation among a multitude of scholarly workers, and on a financial shoestring. It is no secret that proposals to publish the edition were submitted to several university presses and unanimously turned down: it was not until a few of the group of Johnsonian enthusiasts put together a sum from their own pockets by way of guarantee that there was any assurance of the edition's actually achieving print.

The circumstances of its origin account for many of the differences between the Yale edition and some other recent collected editions of noted writers, where assured institutional backing has made possible more rigorous central control of editorial policy, greater supervision of the work of individual editors by the general editorial staff (and hence greater uniformity of editorial practice in the finished product), and a faster and a more efficient production schedule. The Yale Johnson remains a voluntary and co-operative enterprise. All the editorial work has to be done in spare time left over from busy teaching and administrative schedules and other scholarly commitments, except in so far as individuals can persuade their employers and the custodians of research grants to give them occasional freed time or financial assistance (and it has been discovered that research grants are much less easily obtained for editorial work of this kind than for projected critical monographs).[7] In a more "efficiently" run editorial factory, if it looked as though an individual editor had no hope of even approximating a deadline, steps might be taken to replace him,

7 / From time to time, the edition has been able to afford to pay for some released time for the present general editor.

even, if necessary, by someone with inferior qualifications, so as to maintain the publication schedule. This has never been the attitude of the editorial committee of the Yale Johnson. If the person it feels is best qualified to edit *Rasselas*, for example, happens to be the harried chairman of a large university department, it inclines to prefer to wait until he retires from the chairmanship, or perhaps even from university teaching, rather than press him to let some less busy but less experienced scholar take over. (Though a number of "first choices" have nevertheless found it necessary to withdraw because of the pressure of seemingly endless administrative responsibilities.) This policy means, of course, that the estimated date of completion of the Yale Johnson remains anybody's guess. But the advantages of waiting in the expectation that a really mature work of scholarship will eventually see light seems to the group to outweigh those of getting a completed set of "efficiently" but perfunctorily edited volumes on to library shelves. After all, if the world of literary scholarship has managed, with no noticeable impatience, to endure for two hundred years the absence of a competently edited *Rasselas*, another decade or two of waiting will do it no great harm.

The edition was fortunate in securing a fine bibliographical scholar, Allen T. Hazen of Columbia, to preside over its somewhat chaotic birth pangs. Hazen became general editor in 1955. Problems of health forced him to resign this appointment in 1966, when John H. Middendorf, also of Columbia, who had for several years acted as Hazen's able associate editor, replaced him. Fortunately, Hazen's health permits him to continue (in the intervals of completing his monumental catalogue of Horace Walpole's library) to lend his great wisdom in editorial matters to the Johnsonian group. Hazen's attitude toward bibliographical and editorial questions, as those who have attended his courses in bibliography know, has always been the converse of the "Virginia school." His philosophy is an empirical one – "What is the purpose of the edition? How well will it work?"

– rather than one of dogmatic systematization; he sees little point in trying to make descriptive bibliography and editorship exact sciences, even if it were possible to do so. Thus individual editors have had considerable latitude to deal with textual matters in the way that seems best for their individual problems – sometimes to the distress of reviewers. Many of the Johnsonian editors, however, have remained unmoved by such protests: indeed, the editors of the forthcoming three volumes of *The Rambler* have departed so far from the currently hallowed doctrine of reproducing the "accidentals" of the first edition of a work as to take the *fourth* edition as their copy text.[8]

But in any case the voluntary and co-operative nature of the enterprise made it inevitable that there would be more democratic give-and-take than in the work of more tightly controlled editorial projects. (And those who are bothered by the amount of diversity that will be found among the volumes of the Yale Johnson might ask themselves just how much value there would be in trying to maintain rigid uniformity of editorial practice in a multi-volumed edition containing work in an immensely wide variety of genres.) In early meetings of the editors and members of the editorial committee, there was naturally much lively debate about the general editorial principles to be adopted. These questions were decided by majority vote, though perhaps with the tacit understanding that an individual editor who felt strongly that a certain agreed-on general practice was inappropriate to the particular material he was in charge of would be listened to sympathetically when the time came to submit his copy.

It may be useful to describe some of the major decisions that

8 / The controversy will of course continue. But it is well to bear in mind that the procedures by which books came into being in the 1750s were not identical with those of Elizabethan times, and that the information we seek when we examine early editions of a Johnsonian periodical essay is often not the same as that which we seek from the early editions of an Elizabethan play.

were taken. There was virtually unanimous agreement on the opening paragraph of the statement of general editorial rules:

> The purpose of the edition is to produce a sound and readable text of Johnson, for use by graduate students, literary critics, literary scholars, and informed literate readers. It is not planned primarily as a text book for use in secondary schools, or as an exercise in ingenuity of bibliographical annotation.

The word "readable," of course, immediately brought up the question of the amount of modernization of the text to be done. There was little sentiment in favour of an exact reproduction of all the capitalization and italicization found in, say, the style of the *Gentleman's Magazine* of the 1730s and 1740s, where many of Johnson's pieces first appeared. (Though there was some, by those who asked, "What will be the use of the edition, if the really conscientious scholar still feels he cannot completely rely on it for textual study, but must consult the first editions?" The answer is simply that if its main purpose is to get Johnson's writings read by the modern educated public, who would certainly be discouraged by archaic typography, the needs of the specialist scholar must take second place; and if this edition is inadequate to those needs, he will have to continue to seek out the early editions, or perhaps agitate for the publication of facsimile reprints of them.)

On the other hand, those who wished to go the whole way in accepting the implications of "readable," and to print a text completely modernized in spelling, capitalization, and punctuation, were soundly outvoted – though, interestingly, the minority included (as well as the present writer) the grand old man of Johnsonian editing, the late R. W. Chapman of Oxford and the general editor. Chapman even argued for Americanized spelling of words like "labour," on the ground that the edition was, after all, being published by an American press and Americans would form the largest body of its users. But even Chapman's

American associates in the minority group drew back from so "radical" a suggestion, though it might be hard to formulate a convincing reason for their reluctance – it was perhaps simply a feeling that to do so would be impiety to the memory of so sturdy an Englishman as Johnson.[9] The majority view, incorporated into the editorial rules, was thus a compromise between the two extremes: to modernize capitalization and the use of italics, but to preserve the spelling of the copy-text – "Correct only genuine misprints or carelessnesses (like *belieif*), not variants" – and to retain its punctuation "whenever it is clear and correct. Add or alter punctuation only when needed by a modern reader, but do not add or alter merely as a choice. Textual note whenever any change involves two possible interpretations."

Much can be said in favour of this final ruling, as representing the most workable way of achieving readability without completely nullifying the possible utility of the edition to the student of eighteenth-century linguistic usage (though it perhaps needs to be pointed out to the young student that the spelling and punctuation found in the printed copy-texts are at least as likely to represent the compositor's or the printing house's preferences as Johnson's). In practice, however, it has resulted in some problems for editors that perhaps were not anticipated at the time of the vote. "Italics used for dialogue in the copy-text should be changed to quotation marks. Italics used for emphasis in the copy-text should be retained," the present rubric reads. This leaves undetermined the question of what to do with what is perhaps the largest category of italicization in many of the Johnsonian copy-texts – places where it indicates quotation,

9 / For spelling in editorial annotation, the committee decided that the forms preferred by the *Concise Oxford English Dictionary* should be used. Not everyone is completely happy about this rule, which requires, for instance, the spelling *connexion*, which seems to be obsolescent even in England (cf. the 1965 edition of Fowler's *Modern English Usage*).

as in the opening paragraph of *Thoughts on the Coronation of King George III*:

Magnificence in obscurity is equally vain with *a sun-dial in the grave.*

Probably the original intention of the rule was that such instances were to be subsumed under "dialogue." Yet (to this editor at least) it looks obtrusive and ungraceful to put into roman type surrounded by quotation marks the fine phrase from Donne that Johnson italicized:

Magnificence in obscurity is equally vain with "a sun-dial in the grave."

The fact is that mid-twentieth-century usage is still uncertain about what to do in such a case. An undergraduate in an essay for his tutor might use quotation marks in this way (or append a solemn footnote calling attention to the source). A more sophisticated writer, addressing a more urbane audience, might be inclined to leave the quotation unmarked in any way, hoping that the reader will appreciate the compliment to his erudition, or, if he wanted to make sure it was recognized as a quotation, preface it by "(as Donne says)" or the like. Johnson and his contemporaries appear to have found a tactful and satisfying way of dealing with the problem, and it seems a pity to substitute an inferior one for it. Moreover, there are italicized phrases in the early editions where one suspects that Johnson *may* be quoting but cannot run down the source, though on the other hand he *may* simply be italicizing his own words for emphasis. What is the editor to do? The simplest answer seems to be to take advantage of the apparent loophole in the editorial ruling and leave the phrase in italics – a short italicized passage like the one printed above will not greatly diminish its readability for the modern reader.[10]

10 / One of the Yale editors has pointed out to me still another problem: Johnson and his printers used italics for indirect quotation as well as direct,

Similarly with the rule that the use of capital letters is to be modernized: "Use caps only for proper names and personified abstractions." This calls for some tricky decisions by an editor of Johnson's poetry; and there are passages in his prose as well where an abstract noun may or may not be intended to convey some suggestion of personification. It might be argued that the wisest thing to do in such cases is to be conservative – if a capitalized abstract noun in the copy-text could possibly be intended to carry a hint of imagery, retain the capital. But opinions about this differ. Likewise with the rule for punctuation: what should one do with a passage like this: "His [Shakespeare's] adherence to general nature has exposed him to the censure of criticks, who form their judgments upon narrower principles"? Eighteenth-century usage tended to set off all subordinate clauses by commas, without making the modern distinction between non-restrictive (set off) and restrictive ones (not set off). Almost certainly this clause of Johnson's is intended restrictively, and to retain the comma in a modern edition would mislead the modern reader; the editor should surely remove it, appending a note explaining why he did so. But there are other passages where the problem of determining Johnson's intention, and hence the punctuation to be used in a modern edition is more difficult. Here is an example, from a political piece dealing with the relations between Great Britain and her American colonies: "I have not in general a favorable opinion of restraints, which always produce discontent and an habitual violation of laws." Is Johnson saying that he disapproves of *all* restraints on colonies or only of *some*, those which always produce discontent? The answer makes a good deal of difference to one's assessment of Johnson's basic political philosophy; or, con-

e.g., in the *Life of Pope,* "He was asked by his Royal Highness *how he could love a Prince while he disliked Kings*?" Modernization would remove all indication that these are quoted words.

The suggestion was made to the editorial committee that single quotation marks, after the British fashion, be used for quoted material, but it was voted down.

versely, the editor's assessment of that philosophy may well determine how he is going to punctuate the passage for the modern reader.

The rule about textual notes is the sensible one for a "reading" edition, "Textual notes will show variant readings, but this is not an attempt to record all readings of all editions. Therefore, no notes of obvious misprints of no interest, or of obvious corruption in later editions." It has sometimes been hard, however, to persuade budding editors, eager to prove their assiduity in collation, to take this self-denying ordinance seriously; and even after copy and galleys have been drastically pruned, reviewers may still have occasion to complain of otiose textual annotation. It was originally hoped that the mechanics of textual annotation could be kept very simple; but special problems, particularly with texts edited from heavily corrected manuscript, have sometimes necessitated a fair amount of improvised elaboration, not all of it as efficient as one might hope for.

Perhaps no matter has given rise to more diversity of opinion among editors and members of the editorial committee (and reviewers of the volumes already published) than the question of how much explanatory annotation to provide. To begin with, every Johnsonian had before his eyes the awful example of Birkbeck Hill, whose penchant for interminable, gossipy, irrelevant annotation culminated in the quite grotesque apparatus of his three-volume edition of *The Lives of the Poets* in 1905. He is properly held up, in the editorial instructions for the Yale edition, as an illustration of what is to be avoided:

> Notes should not become merely exclamatory, laudatory, or discursive. There should be no references to monographs on matters mentioned incidentally in the text. For example, Hill's notes on the first page of his edition of SJ's *Annals* (in [*Johnsonian*] *Miscellanies*) are interesting in themselves, certainly to Hill and doubtless to many others, but they do not elucidate SJ's autobiography:
>
> Franklin's letter to his wife concerning change in calendar

The year 1709 a year of great dearth according to Adam Smith's tabulation of wheat prices
[On "man-midwife"] *accoucheur* is not in SJ's *Dictionary,* and citation from *Tristram Shandy*
The baptism of SJ's father

The "encyclopaedic" annotation of the Yale edition of Horace Walpole's correspondence is likewise rejected: "No note for a person in *DNB* unless his identification is immediately useful in comprehending the allusion. Thus, no notes for a reference to Pope or Spenser." What *should* be done is described in an admirably lucid statement which begins, "Before writing footnotes, try to imagine a user who starts to read SJ, perhaps in Australia, fifty years hence."

Nevertheless, for all the very sensible guidance provided here, it has become clear that each editor has his own pet philosophy of footnoting, which he holds very firmly, which corresponds exactly to that of no other editor, and which no amount of argument can shake. No doubt as a natural reaction to the example of Hill, some editorial work that has been published calls attention with a certain air of complacency to the "leanness" of its annotation, a quality which a number of reviewers have seen no reason to applaud. Certainly, to annotate *The Rambler,* for example, with complete thoroughness – to try to discover Johnson's sources for the philosophical, moral, and theological ideas expressed in it, to note the many parallels to them in other works of Johnson and the many echoes in his writing from other writers – would be a tremendously taxing job, the work of a great many years of patient research. Some feel, however, that it needs eventually to be done; perhaps in time a scholar will be found who is willing to give the best years of his life to the task of producing the "definitively" annotated edition of *The Rambler.* Meanwhile, the Yale edition will at least provide an adequate text and explain the more prominent allusions. When one comes to Johnson's political writings, however, it seems clear that the modern reader, unless he is a trained historian of the period, cannot follow many of them with any real comprehension unless a thorough description of the background of political history which gave rise to each piece is provided. This the Yale edition of the political writings will attempt to do. But even here the question of what the hypothetical Australian reader half a century from now may be expected to take judicial notice of cannot always be easily answered. The term "Jacobitism" must come up frequently in any account of the background of Johnson's earlier political writings. Is an editor safe in trying to elucidate it by the comment, which many recent historians have found useful, that the role played by "Jacobitism" in English politics of the first half of the eighteenth century was closely analogous to that played by "communism" in American politics from the 1920s to the present? Or will allusions to the Cold War have become meaningless to the Australian reader of the year 2000? The editorial committee is still debating this one, with strong convictions on both sides of the question.[11]

11 / The editorial committee recently formally resolved that it "feels that evanescent modern political references in the introduction and annotation should be eschewed." This is no doubt an excellent ideal; but what is "evanescent"? A reference to the question currently being argued in the law courts of the United States, whether there is a right of appeal to any other body from the decision of the house of representatives to exclude an elected member, Adam Clayton Powell? It happens to be precisely the question argued by Johnson, with reference to the house of commons, in *The False Alarm*, 1770. A reference to current protests about the censorship of the London stage by the Lord Chamberlain's office? These protests have continued to be made ever since the publication of the earliest and most violent of them, Johnson's *A Compleat Vindication of the Licensers of the Stage*, 1739. Matters which have been hotly debated throughout the two centuries since Johnson wrote about them and are still far from being finally adjudicated can hardly be called "evanescent"; and to ignore their currency and treat them as though they were dead issues – as has often been done in critical studies of Johnson, and as the committee's resolution seems to recommend be done – is a piece of critical falsification.

Judging from his own literary practice, it seems unlikely that Johnson would have been in favour of such academic detachment. The fact is that almost every one of the political questions that concerned Johnson –

An account of some of the individual pieces of editing that have been completed and some that still have to be completed will illustrate the bewildering variety of problems encountered in the task of trying to prepare a satisfactory edition of Johnson's writings. Volume I of the Yale edition (*Diaries, Prayers, Annals,* edited by E. L. McAdam, Jr., with Donald and Mary Hyde) appeared in 1958, only a year or two after the organization of the edition got under way. There was nothing miraculous in this speed: for many years Professor McAdam and Mr. and Mrs. Hyde had been preparing their edition of Johnson's private papers for independent publication, and generously consented to allow it to form part of the edition. The laborious work of collecting, deciphering, and arranging the fragmentary remains of Johnson's voluminous diaries – shortly before his death he made a holocaust of them – is an epic in itself, which it is impossible to discuss fully here. As well as recovering and printing for the first time much new material, the editors have made invaluable contributions to the study of Johnson by restoring important passages which had been falsified by earlier editors – notably the Reverend George Strahan, who, in his anxiety to project an image of Johnson that would cause no scandal to the weaker brethren, vigorously scratched out, in the manuscript, such passages as this, where Johnson dwells on the memory of his dead wife, Tetty: "On what we did amiss, and our faults were great, I have thought of late with more regret than at any former time. She was, I think, very penitent. May God have accepted her repentance; may he accept mine." Some of these were recovered by the use of infra-red ray photography; others, where the crosshatching was deeper, have not yet been and perhaps never will be.[12] Boswell, too, did his share of remaking

---

nationalism, colonialism, the consequences of Negro slavery and the ill-treatment of non-European races by European and American colonists, the dangers of political partisanship and political cant – is still with us and likely to be with us for a long time, as indeed Johnson foresaw.

12 / Since this was written, J. D. Fleeman has published a remarkable article (*Review of English Studies,* May 1968), reporting dozens of new

Johnson after his own image, following Strahan in silently omitting from Johnson's last prayer, on his deathbed, the important petition "Forgive and accept my late conversion" (presumably because this would make Johnson seem too much of – horrors! – an "Evangelical"), and from one of Johnson's diaries the memorandum on the first anniversary of Tetty's death that he proposed to set out the next day in search of a second wife (Johnson's single-minded devotion to Tetty was a striking trait of the Boswellian "Johnson," and must not be interfered with). Unlike Strahan, however, Boswell did not attempt to destroy the evidence: the authentic text of the last prayer remained available to the public in Hawkins's *Life*, and Boswell's transcription of the passage about the second wife, although concealed in his papers for a century and a half, was not blotted out. Distortions like these have been rectified by the new edition.

In printing the diaries, the editors were faced with a difficult problem of explanatory annotation. Such a great deal of it was necessary to make Johnson's jottings comprehensible that the usual method of keying separate footnotes to superior numbers in the text would have resulted in an unbearably cluttered page. Instead of footnotes, then, the editors supplied in the bottom half of each page a running "commentary," which in effect translated the entries in the text into a brief narrative of what Johnson was doing during the periods the entries recorded. Some readers were alarmed by this audacious innovation, but it is hard to think of what better way the text could be made intelligible. A second edition (1960), with some small corrections, has already been published.

Volume II (1963; *The Idler*, edited by W. J. Bate and J. M. Bullitt of Harvard, and Johnson's contributions to *The Adventurer*, edited by L. F. Powell of Oxford) presented only the perennial questions of what copy-text to use (*The Idler* followed that of the second edition – i.e., the first collected edition, rather than the original printings of the essays in the *Universal Chron-*

---

readings in Johnson's "Prayers and Meditations" obtained by a closer inspection, in ordinary light, of the manuscript.

icle – and was chastised for doing so), how much explanatory annotation to provide (that of *The Idler* was "lean"), and how the authorship of the various essays in *The Adventurer* was to be assigned (most Johnsonians have been willing to follow Powell's conclusions, though the question is still being debated).[13] Volumes III, IV, and V, containing *The Rambler*, are in type and awaiting final revision of proofs before going to press. The textual editor, Albrecht Strauss of the University of North Carolina, has taken as his copy-text that of the fourth edition (London, 1756). As he points out, Johnson did not read proof on the first edition – the individual folio numbers, published each Tuesday and Saturday from 1750 to 1752 and often composed in great haste – and it is hard to say what advantage would accrue from following the accidentals of the 1750–52 folios rather than those of the 1756 edition. Johnson had, however, made a great many substantive revisions to the text by the time of the 1756 edition (the last which he revised), and, as Strauss says, "The choice of this edition makes for very substantial convenience in the treatment of a complicated textual history and reduces the risk of editorial error."[14] The

13 / *The Idler* presented a problem in numbering. The original weekly issues were numbered from 1 to 104. When they were first published in collected form (1761), however, no. 22, a scarifying, Swiftian satire on human warfare, was dropped, and the remainder renumbered, ending with 103. Later reprints retained this numbering, but sometimes added the original no. 22 after 103. The Yale edition, no doubt sensibly, keeps the revised numbering, which has become traditional, though the student has to be warned to distinguish between "*Idler* no. 22" (originally no. 23) and "Original *Idler* no. 22." Johnson's *Sermons* presented a similar problem: should the traditional numbering (1 to 25) of the *Sermons Left for Publication by John Taylor* be retained, or should a more rational, chronologically ordered numbering be adopted by the Yale editors? Again, it was decided to keep the traditional numbering, if only because references in articles and monographs have made use of it for a century or more.

14 / Strauss gives a convincing justification of his practice in his lively article "The Dull Duty of an Editor: On Editing the Text of Johnson's *Rambler*," *The Bookmark* (Friends of the University of North Carolina Library), June, 1965. Another editorial problem he discusses is whether the Latin text of the epigraphs of the *Ramblers* should be corrected to agree with accepted modern texts of Horace, Juvenal, and the rest. Is a variant

textual apparatus of course records the many substantive variants from the 1750–52 London folio edition, the 1750–52 Edinburgh edition printed by Elphinston (though the authority of its variants now seems dubious), and the 1752 London collected edition. Interestingly, it was discovered in the process of collation that a number of substantive, "stop-press" variants occur among different copies of the individual 1750–52 London folio *Ramblers*; these too are of course recorded in the Yale apparatus. The spelling in the 1756 *Rambler* is quite erratic – "public" and "publick," "persue" and "pursue," "choose" and "chuse" impartially alternate (though that of the first – folio – edition is even more erratic). These variants presumably represent merely the preferences of different compositors, or perhaps Johnson's own inconsistencies; it was felt that they would not greatly distract the modern reader, and general editorial policy of the edition directs that they be retained. Explanatory annotation, for which W. J. Bate was responsible, continues to be "lean."

Volume VI (1964; the *Poems*, edited by E. L. McAdam, Jr., with George Milne) involved more problems than might have been expected, considering that the edition of Johnson's poems by Nichol Smith and McAdam had appeared only a little more than twenty years earlier. But during that time a good deal had taken place. Johnson's holographs of *The Vanity of Human Wishes*, part of *London*, and a draft of *Irene* had turned up, with a wealth of earlier readings. A new theatrical prologue – that to Garrick's early farce, *Lethe* – had been discovered by Mary Knapp in the Folger Library, making six in all. So had the complete text of Johnson's juvenile verse-translation of Addison's Latin poem, *The Battle of the Cranes and Pygmies* (in

---

reading encountered in a *Rambler* motto a printer's mistake, or the result of Johnson's quoting from memory, or an accepted variant in an eighteenth-century or earlier edition of the Latin author? (Surely if the variant was not a printer's error but something Johnson intended, whether a misquotation or not, it should be retained; a footnote may call attention to the discrepancy.)

which, he ruefully told Boswell, he had perpetrated the Irish bull, "Down from the guardian boughs the nests they flung, / And kill'd the yet unanimated young," though the manuscript shows "kill'd" corrected to "crush'd"). Most striking was a wealth of juvenilia which had been preserved among the Boswell papers, including Johnson's earliest known English poem, written when he was about fifteen, and entitled – how Wordsworth would have stared! – "On a Daffodil: the First Flower the Author Had Seen That Year." These additions, together with the arrangement of poems in strict chronological order – the 1941 volume preserved the traditional but irrational order of the older collections, beginning with *London* and *The Vanity of Human Wishes*, followed by the prologues – should help to convince doubters how very close poetry was to Johnson throughout his creative life, especially at its beginning and at its end, when he beguiled his sleeplessness by translating those highly "romantic" productions, the epigrams of the Greek anthology, into euphonious Latin verse.

The publication of volumes VII and VIII, at the time this is being written, has just been announced. They contain the Yale edition's attempt to present in manageable form the bulk of Johnson's critical and editorial work on Shakespeare. As the editor, Arthur Sherbo of Michigan State University, has pointed out, it is not Johnson's beautifully written but not very original *Preface* that best exhibits Johnson's greatness as a critic, but his detailed annotation of the Shakespearian plays, which shows us his criticism "in operation." The ideal way to consult this is, of course, in its original format – *in situ*, at the foot of the page of the Shakespearian text with which it deals, and intermingled with the notes of earlier critics which Johnson selected for inclusion here (for Johnson's was the earliest variorum edition of Shakespeare). Any other method is bound to introduce some distortion. But the prospect of reprinting the eight volumes of the 1765 or the ten of the 1773 edition was a formidable one. There was much debate about how much to reprint, and the decisions urged ranged from "print everything" to "print only Johnson's most distinguished critical contributions." The present edition is admittedly a compromise with the problem of bulk – only enough of the Shakespearian text is given along with each Johnsonian note to make it intelligible, and only those non-Johnsonian notes (usually summarized) which Johnson supplemented or commented on. It might be argued that Johnson's selection of notes by earlier editors was in itself an operation of his critical judgment, and to make a really accurate assessment of that judgment all those other notes should be available; perhaps one of the reprint firms now flourishing will be inspired to get out a facsimile of one of the important early editions. But the two Yale volumes will certainly provide a far more valid picture of Johnson's Shakespearian criticism than the selection on which most modern students of Johnson have hitherto relied: Raleigh's niggardly, capricious, and inaccurate *Johnson on Shakespeare* (1908).[15] They also include important Shakespearian criticism by Johnson apart from the edition – the *Miscellaneous Observations on Macbeth* (1745), the dedication of Charlotte Lennox's *Shakespeare Illustrated* (1753), the two sets of *Proposals* for an edition – and, of course, give the highly important variants that Johnson introduced into his successive revised editions of the plays. Bertrand H. Bronson, of the University of California, Berkeley, provides an informative and appreciative introduction to the two volumes.

As might have been anticipated, most of the editorial assignments which were made when the edition was planned, some ten years ago, have been completed nearly simultaneously, with the result that a considerable backlog of completed copy exists, at the press or on the desk of the general editor, in various stages of "processing." These manuscripts will be printed more or less

15 / As Sherbo has pointed out, Raleigh, among other things, prints notes from the first edition that Johnson modified or discarded in later editions, and once prints as Johnson's a long note by Warburton; modern anthologists of Johnson, instead of consulting the Johnsonian text, have taken over these errors from Raleigh.

in order of receipt. Galley proofs have just been received for volume IX,[16] *A Journey to the Western Islands of Scotland*, edited by Mary Lascelles of Oxford. Volume X should be *Political Writings*, which I am editing. It includes the two violent anti-Walpolian pamphlets of 1739, *Marmor Norfolciense* and *A Compleat Vindication of the Licensers of the Stage*; a group of pieces, most of them printed in the *Literary Magazine*, 1756, on matters connected with the Seven Years' War (to which Johnson objected as vigorously as some readers of this essay object to the war in Vietnam, and for very similar reasons); the four pamphlets of the 1770s in defence of policies of the Grafton and North ministries, *The False Alarm*, *Thoughts on . . . Falkland's Islands*, *The Patriot*, and *Taxation No Tyranny*; and a selection of smaller, mostly journalistic, pieces having some political reference. A really complete collection of Johnson's writings having a marked political content would include *London*, various *Idlers*, the *Life of Cheynel*, a sizable part of the *Life of Milton*, and others; it would also include the multi-volumed *Parliamentary Debates*, described below. The myth, originating with Macaulay and parroted by some later writers, that Johnson was essentially apolitical is perhaps the most fantastic of the various nineteenth-century Johnson myths: few, if any, major English writers have been more politically committed and politically knowledgeable, or readier to write on political matters, than Johnson. The rationale of the present volume, however,

16 / The numbering is tentative. John M. Robson has commented (*Editing Nineteenth-Century Texts*, Toronto, 1967, pp. 106–7), "One could, of course, simply number the volumes [of a multi-volumed edition] in the order of their appearance. . . . The current Yale edition of Samuel Johnson's works seems to have been started on this principle (or lack of principle), with slightly unfortunate results." This is not quite an accurate description of what has been done, as the appearance of volume VI in 1964 testifies. But in any case one wonders just what the unfortunate results have been. Johnson's private diaries seem an admirable choice for volume I. True, *The Idler* and *The Adventurer* (volume II) might perhaps have appeared more appropriately after rather than before *The Rambler*. At the time they were ready for publication, however, it was not certain how many volumes *The Rambler* would run to.

has been merely to include writings with a political content not subsumed under other established categories of Johnson's works – the poems, periodical essays, biographies, and so on. To make many of these intelligible to the modern reader, fairly extensive annotation dealing with their background of political history seemed advisable.

Extensive annotation of theological matters also seemed desirable in the edition of Johnson's fine, and neglected, *Sermons*, prepared by Jean Hagstrum (Northwestern) and James Gray (Bishop's University). Problems of identification arise here: Johnson's friend and biographer, Sir John Hawkins, reported that Johnson had composed some forty sermons for ecclesiastical friends, charging two guineas each for his services. Twenty-five were published after Johnson's death under the ambiguous title *Sermons Left for Publication by John Taylor*, Johnson's intimate friend from schoolboy days, later rector of Market Bosworth, Derbyshire, and of St. Margaret's, Westminster, and prebendary of Westminster Abbey. One of these in its entirety and portions of another, however, Hagstrum believes not to be Johnson's. In addition we have a charity sermon preached at St. Paul's Cathedral in 1745 by another friend, the Reverend Henry Hervey Aston, which was shown some time ago by L. F. Powell to be by Johnson; one composed for the Reverend William Dodd to be delivered at Newgate shortly before his execution for forgery – Johnson's strenuous efforts to win a pardon for Dodd have been regarded by legal historians as a landmark in the campaign for the mitigation of English criminal law in the eighteenth century;[17] and one in manuscript in the Yale library, which Johnson may also have com-

17 / See Leon Radzinowicz, *A History of English Criminal Law and Its Administration from 1750: The Movement for Reform, 1750–1833* (1948), chapter XIV, "Growth of Public Uneasiness: The Case of Dr. Dodd." Radzinowicz also pays tribute to the role played by Johnson's *Rambler* and *Idler* essays in the reform of criminal law in his chapter X, "Some Expressions of Doubt as to the Merits of the Penal System: Dr. Johnson." Johnson's writings on Dodd's behalf, a dozen or more items, will form a separate section in the Yale edition.

posed for Taylor. The rest of the forty are still unidentified but some of them may still turn up: for instance, a sermon or sermons composed, according to Mrs. Thrale, for his young friend the Reverend George Strahan, and a November 5 sermon preached at "St. James's (or some other capital city pulpit [?St. Margaret's, Westminster]) . . . and afterwards published by command of the Archbishop."

Nearing completion also is the volume containing Johnson's early translation, or rather adaptation, of Joachim Le Grand's French version of Father Jeronymo Lobo's early seventeenth-century *A Voyage to Abyssinia*, together with Le Grand's own "dissertations" on questions raised by Lobo's book, now edited by Joel Gold, of the University of Kansas. This very substantial volume – usually dismissed as a trivial piece of hack-work by earlier students, many of whom probably never even looked at it – is now taken very seriously as evidence of Johnson's early interest in certain complex and controversial religious and political questions, in particular the question of the treatment of the natives of remote countries by European colonizers and proselytizers. The Jesuit mission to "convert" Ethiopia, in which Lobo played an important part, was seen by Protestant controversialists (and by Johnson) as a facet of Portuguese imperial and commercial expansion – Ethiopia was from early times, and still is, a Christian country. The edition will also illustrate Johnson's very free methods of "translation" from the French – he never hesitates to abridge, expand, or paraphrase the original when he feels the need to do so, sometimes in a quite tendentious manner.

One of the most difficult editorial assignments was that assumed by Benjamin Hoover of Brandeis, to put into readable and intelligible form the three years or more of Johnson's "Debates in the Senate of Magna Lilliputia" – the *Gentleman's Magazine*'s ingenious device (the idea may have been Johnson's own) for evading the official ban on reporting the debates of the parliament of Great Britain. Again, earlier students of Johnson have tended to dismiss these slightingly (thus, of course, escaping the onerous task of studying them). But they are an important incident in his career. They are still consulted, in Cobbett's *Parliamentary History* (the predecessor of Hansard) and other collections, as the quasi-official records of the debates of the times; indeed, incautious historians still sometimes quote passages of Johnsonian prose as testimony to Pitt's or Chesterfield's breadth of mind and command of English rhetoric. Perhaps more immediately important for Johnson, they placed the journal for which he worked and which at times he probably edited, the *Gentleman's Magazine*, in a secure financial position and gave it prestige. The general public were intensely interested in the hectic parliamentary contests of the years that preceded Walpole's downfall, and it was audacious and foresighted – "democratic," indeed – of the journal to risk prosecution to provide it with these reports (which, beneath the veneer of Johnsonian prose, are reasonably accurate accounts of what was said in parliament). It is an interesting reflection that the first "magazine" in history, the *Gentleman's*, was probably also the most successful – it was published continuously from 1731 to 1907 – and Johnson had much to do with laying the foundation for its success.

Hoover's editorial task, now nearing completion, has not been an enviable one. A great deal of research into the minutiae of political history and biography of the time has been necessary to provide the explanatory annotation to make the work comprehensible by the modern reader. The problem of identifying Johnson's share in the debates is formidable, and will perhaps never be solved with complete certainty. Tradition has it that two other writers contributed to them besides Johnson – William Guthrie, his predecessor, and John Hawkesworth, his successor. But where one finished and another began is difficult to determine; little reliable evidence other than internal is available. Moreover, there is the complication that Johnson is said to have revised some of Guthrie's reports for publication; if these could be identified, should they be included in the edition or not? To make matters worse, it has recently been argued that Johnson's contributions to the *Debates* extend virtually a year beyond the date hitherto accepted for their termination: should these recently attributed debates be included or not? They could swell the bulk of the edition by almost another volume. A satisfactory compromise might be to include them in smaller type as an appendix, so that students will at least have the text available to assist them in making up their minds whether or not they are by Johnson. It is understandable that, given problems of this kind – problems often encountered in connection with other journalistic work by Johnson as well – a number of Johnsonian students have recently turned their attention to the study of modern techniques of statistical analysis of style, and considerable quantities of Johnsonian and near-Johnsonian prose have already been run through computers in the hope of finding criteria of Johnsonian authorship that can be quantitatively assessed. What success will be achieved by these techniques only the future can tell.

It was thought to begin with that the textual editing of the *Debates* would present no great problem: there is only one authoritative text for them, that of the *Gentleman's Magazine*, and the editor's only task would be to modernize it and correct obvious misprints. It was presently discovered, however, that it is not quite so simple as that. "The text of the *Gentleman's Magazine*" is a misnomer: it turns out that the periodical was so popular that the early numbers in particular were often reprinted, with inevitable textual variants, and there is frequently no obvious way of discovering whether a given copy is the original printing or a reprint. The same problem exists for other Johnsonian pieces whose first edition is that of the *Gentleman's Magazine*. The present writer encountered it while editing, for the volume of *Political Writings*, Johnson's "A Debate Between the Committee of the House of Commons in 1657 and Oliver Cromwell," a skilful condensation of a Restoration pamphlet. I had transcribed the text of the first part of it from the February 1741 number of the *Gentleman's Magazine* in the University of Toronto central library. Some time later I checked my transcription against a copy of the same number in the Yale University library, and was horrified to find the transcription full of careless mistakes – "compiled" for "complied," "change" for "charge," "individious" for "invidious," "viligent" for "vigilant," and the like. If my ability to transcribe was no better than this, I decided, I had better abandon all thoughts of setting up as an editor. Fortunately for my peace of mind, when I had a chance to examine the Toronto file of the *Gentleman's Magazine* again, I found that the transcription *was* accurate – all its aberrations were faithful reproductions of the Toronto copy; the Yale copy was a different, more correct setting of the same February 1741 number of the *Magazine*. It will probably not be necessary, however, to embark on the Herculean task of collating the hundreds of extant runs of the *Gentleman's Magazine*. W. B. Todd has recently done useful work in locating identifying marks for the various reprints of early numbers of the *Magazine*; and in any case, the variants seem to be mostly the harmless sort of misspellings noted above, which would be routinely corrected in the normal process of editing, not serious substantive changes to the author's text, so that, even though a Yale editor declines to check his text against every copy of the *Gentleman's Magazine* in the world, no great misrepresentation of Johnson's intentions is likely to occur. (At least, one hopes so!)

If the *Debates*, as seems likely, will fill three volumes, a total of fifteen volumes of the Yale edition are either already published or in the final stages of preparation. A great deal more of the Johnsonian *œuvre* remains to be edited and even to be assigned to editors. In some cases, the editors appointed have become involved in heavy administrative and other duties, and one can only hope that in time some relief from these duties will permit them to return to Johnson. *Rasselas*, in the care of Gwin

Kolb, of the University of Chicago, and Robert Metzdorf, now a professional bibliographer in New York, is one of these. The heavy responsibility for *The Lives of the Poets*[18] was originally given to F. W. Hilles, who later became chairman of the English department at Yale, and W. R. Keast, then of Cornell. Keast's involvement in administration, culminating in his appointment as a university president, forced him to withdraw from the edition (another similar loss to administration was Robert W. Rogers of Illinois, who was originally appointed to edit the Lobo-Le Grand *Voyage to Abyssinia*). Hilles's retirement from university teaching has fortunately enabled him now to turn his whole attention to the *Lives*; moreover certain important lives are being edited by specialist scholars – Clarence Tracy of Acadia University for the *Life of Savage* and Henry Pettit of the University of Colorado for the *Life of Young*, to mention two.

Some other works present peculiarly difficult problems. The editing of the Vinerian lectures in English law (*c.* 1766), in which Johnson afforded substantial assistance to his friend Sir Robert Chambers, the second Vinerian professor at Oxford (in succession to the great Blackstone, whose lectures constitute his famous *Commentaries*), involves that of trying to distinguish the Johnsonian contributions from those of Chambers. The manuscript of the lectures, in the British Museum – some 1,600 pages in a clerical hand – gives no assistance. E. L. McAdam, who brought the work to notice, has isolated certain passages that sound convincingly Johnsonian,[19] and it is easy to agree with him that Johnson's prose style is strikingly different from Chambers's. Yet, as in all such cases, one is never completely sure. Ideally, the solution would be for the Yale edition to print all 1,600 pages, and let the reader make his own decisions. This

18 / Hallowed by time as this title has become, its authority is not certain, and it often misleads young students – sometimes mature scholars as well – as to Johnson's purpose in the work. It would be a bold but might be a salutary action on the part of the Yale editors to restore the original title, *Prefaces, Biographical and Critical, to the Works of the English Poets.*

19 / In his *Dr. Johnson and the English Law* (1951).

seems impracticable; and yet one hesitates to treat the text with less than the full respect due to a work in which some of Johnson's most profound statements of basic moral and political principles are to be found. Johnson's translation of Jean-Pierre Crousaz's *Commentary* on Pope's *Essay on Man* (1739), which includes a retranslation into English prose of Du Resnel's French verse translation of Pope's poem, and a good deal of caustic annotation by Johnson, presents the same problem as the Vinerian lectures and the Shakespeare criticism: how much to print. All? Some? If some, what part? (Matthew Hodgart, of the University of Sussex, has this work in hand.) As for the immense *Dictionary of the English Language*, the Yale editorial committee threw up its collective hands in despair, and decided to do nothing about it (apart, of course, from the *Plan* of the *Dictionary* and the *Preface*, to be edited by James P. Sledd and Gwin Kolb). The recent publication of a facsimile of the first edition (1755) by a commercial reprint house has mitigated some of the unhappiness of Johnsonian scholars at this decision. Yet something should be done at some time to record the many and very important revisions Johnson made to the *Dictionary* between his first edition and his last (1773).

Even when all these projects have been completed – perhaps another six or seven volumes – there remains a large, amorphous mass of minor but by no means negligible writings by Johnson, which may well prove the most difficult editorial task of all: his vast journalistic output of reviews, "letters to the editor," editorial statements, monthly "features" in the *Gentleman's Magazine* and *Literary Magazine*, short biographies, occasional pamphlets, such as those arguing for semicircular rather than elliptical arches in the design of the new Blackfriars bridge and expounding to the Lords Commissioners of the Admiralty Zachariah Williams's method of determining the longitude at sea; his contributions to the works of others – prefaces, dedications, introductory paragraphs, and the like. The canonical problem here is formidable: the number of attributions to Johnson, some probable, some highly improbable, some betwixt-and-between, of short journalistic pieces and the like, made in the last twenty-five years, is startlingly large. If a liberal attitude to such attributions is adopted, the bulk and the editorial labour of the remaining volumes will be great. And yet a liberal attitude seems required: since most of these recently attributed pieces are difficult of access for the ordinary student, an effort should be made to reprint the texts of as many of them as possible – in an appendix, if desired, with no commitment on the part of the editors as to their authenticity, but at least available for study and assessment. And then, finally, will come the mind-boggling task of preparing index volumes for the whole edition – though fortunately the decision was taken to include indexes for the individual volumes or groups of volumes. As was said above, the date when the whole project will be finished remains anyone's guess; it may well turn out that it will be completed by a wholly new generation of scholars from that which initiated it. But it will continue to present a dazzling variety of editorial problems, which, exasperating though they may be, at least ensure that the work will never be boring, "dull." Some – let us hope we shall not be set down as masochists – even find it, on the whole, fun.

Is all this consumption of time and energy and expense, this vast museum of editorial headaches, worth the while? Why bother trying to rescue from oblivion the notes on Crousaz, the Lobo translation, the Vinerian lectures, the chapter (entitled "Being, in the Author's Opinion, the Best Chapter in This History") contributed to Charlotte Lennox's novel *The Female Quixote*? Johnsonians have no doubt about the answers to these questions. The pieces rescued from oblivion are, in fact, full of delight and instruction: nothing that Johnson wrote is without some spark from his inquiring intellect, some touch of distinction from his sense of style. When the twenty-five or more volumes of the Yale edition, flanked by the *Dictionary*, occupy the shelves of the world's libraries, the persistent Macaulayan image of Johnson as a comic old curiosity, whose only interest is as the central character of Boswell's great work of art, should at last disappear. So, too, should the modern practice of "summing up" Johnson's mind and art in a slim, glib volume based on a rapid reading of the usual half-dozen anthology titles and a complacent ignorance of two-thirds or more of what he wrote. Johnson will be seen (as he was by his contemporaries) as one of the really major figures of English literary history, a Colossus bestriding the world of eighteenth-century literature and thought, and the serious critical study of his achievement can at last begin.[20]

20 / The responsibility for errors, omissions, and misjudgments in this paper continues to be mine. But I must acknowledge a debt of gratitude to the many workers on the Yale edition who, in the generous tradition of co-operation among Johnsonians, took the trouble to read an earlier draft of it and purge it of many mistakes, misapprehensions, and carelessnesses.

Members of the Conference

John D. Baird, *Victoria College, University of Toronto*
Theodore Besterman, *Institut Voltaire, Geneva*
O M Brack, Jr, *University of Iowa*
John Carroll, *University College, University of Toronto*
Emily Cloyd, *University of Michigan*
Kathleen Coburn, *Victoria College, University of Toronto*
Beatrice Corrigan, *University of Toronto*
Douglas Creighton, *University of Western Ontario*
E. J. Devereux, *University of Western Ontario*
Donald D. Eddy, *Cornell University*
R. Emerson, *University of Western Ontario*
Norman Endicott, *University College, University of Toronto*
D. G. Esplin, *University of Toronto Library*
George Falle, *Trinity College, University of Toronto*
Michel Gaulin, *Carleton University*
Frederick Gerson, *New College, University of Toronto*
V. E. Graham, *University College, University of Toronto*
Francess Halpenny, *University of Toronto Press*
J. J. Hamm, *Queen's University*
Joyce Hemlow, *McGill University*

Patricia Hernlund, *Wayne State University*
Wm. J. Howard, *St. Michael's College, University of Toronto*
P. Hughes, *Victoria College, University of Toronto*
Roy R. Johnson, *Laurentian University*
Eugène Joliat, *University College, University of Toronto*
E. H. King, *Sudbury*
Douglas Lochhead, *Massey College, University of Toronto*
John McClelland, *Victoria College, University of Toronto*
Kenneth Maclean, *Victoria College, University of Toronto*
P. Moes, *Scarborough College, University of Toronto*
L. J. Morrissey, *University of Western Ontario*
H. S. Noce, *University of Toronto*
Sister Marion Norman, *Loretto College, University of Toronto*
W. A. Oliver, *New College, University of Toronto*
W. J. B. Owen, *McMaster University*
Charles Pullen, *Queen's University*
John Robson, *Victoria College, University of Toronto*
Themistocles Rodis, *Baldwin-Wallace College*
William S. Rogers, *Trinity College, University of Toronto*
C. D. Rouillard, *University College, University of Toronto*
R. M. Schoeffel, *University of Toronto Press*
P. D. Seary, *University College, University of Toronto*
A. Silber, *Victoria College, University of Toronto*
D. I. B. Smith, *University College, University of Toronto*
Samuel S. B. Taylor, *McMaster University*
Clara Thomas, *York University*
L. H. Thoburn, *Laurentian University*
Robert L. Walters, *University of Western Ontario*
Milton Wilson, *Trinity College, University of Toronto*
James F. Woodruff, *University College, University of Toronto*

Index